Fun & Rowdy

Games, Songs, and Activities to Energize Your Youth Group

Group
Loveland, Colorado

Fun & Rowdy

Copyright © 1997 Group Publishing, Inc.

Credits

Contributing Authors: Michelle Anthony, Jody Brolsma, Michael W. Capps, Nanette Goings, Cindy S. Hansen, Christina I. Medina, and Michael Warren
Music Arranger and Engraver: Sylvester Polk
Book Acquisitions Editor: Amy Simpson
Editor: Pamela J. Shoup
Managing Editor: Michael D. Warden
Chief Creative Officer: Joani Schultz
Copy Editor: Debbie Gowensmith
Art Director: Lisa Chandler
Cover Art Director: Helen H. Lannis
Computer Graphic Artist: Joyce Douglas
Cover Designer: Diana Walters
Production Manager: Gingar Kunkel

Unless otherwise noted, Scriptures quoted from The Youth Bible, New Century Version, copyright © 1991 by Word Publishing, Dallas, Texas 75039. Used by permission.

Library of Congress Cataloging-in-Publication Data
 Fun & rowdy : games, songs, and activities to energize your youth
    group / [contributing authors, Michelle Anthony ... [et al.] ;
    editor, Pamela J. Shoup].
           p.   cm.
       ISBN 1-55945-475-X
       1. Church group work with youth. 2. Christian education—Activity
    programs. I. Anthony, Michelle. II. Shoup, Pamela J.
    BV4447.F85 1997
    259' .23--dc21   96-49544
                                                            CIP

10 9 8 7 6 5 4 3 2 1   06 05 04 03 02 01 00 99 98 97
Printed in the United States of America.

Table of Contents

Introduction

Since the title of this book was attractive enough to make you pick it up, you're probably looking for something really fun for your teenagers to do at youth meetings or classes.

Do your kids like to sing? Well … maybe some of them like to sing. Do they like to get up and move around? Sure! Do they like to play games? Always!

With Group's Fun & Rowdy, a book of songs, games, and activities, you'll involve every one of your teenagers in singing, dancing, playing games, and learning from the Bible.

Fun & Rowdy is a *must* for youth ministers, youth group leaders and volunteers, Sunday school teachers, and choir directors. There are a lot of song books out there, but Fun & Rowdy is totally unique. This book combines the following features:

● **Twenty-five "fun and rowdy" songs** are gathered here. Some you'll recognize as traditional hymns and spirituals set to new, energetic arrangements, and others are by contemporary Christian writers and singers including Amy Grant, Steven Curtis Chapman, Newsboys, Wes King, and Audio Adrenaline. All are guaranteed to get teenagers up out of their chairs and moving, stomping their feet, and motioning along with the words.

● **Detailed actions for songs** include circle- and line-dancing, or kids can act out words to the songs using their hands and feet. Teenagers won't be able to sit still when they see the exciting and creative motions they'll learn to do for each song. It makes singing ten times more fun! As a bonus, many songs have variation ideas that offer new experiences every time you sing the songs!

● **More than fifty active games**—both "just-for-fun" and "learning" games—that follow the theme of each song will have your kids throwing Hula Hoops over playground equipment, navigating mazes, playing Bible trivia, or making masks to express themselves.

● **Solid Bible learning** is elemental to many games. Teenagers explore and discuss Scripture in activities, from making mud mortar as the captive Israelites did to spreading the news of the Resurrection as Mary did upon discovering the empty tomb.

● **Piano accompaniment and guitar chords** supplement each song in Fun & Rowdy, so you can play along on instruments as kids sing. Or if you're not very musical, have your church musicians play the songs as you tape-record them for use in your meetings any time!

Go ahead and browse through this book. You'll find a variety of tools you can use to help your teenagers learn more about Bible truths while they worship God and just have fun together. You'll discover a lot of ways you can use Fun & Rowdy. Here are some ideas to add to your own:

● Sing the songs and do the motions to open or close your youth meetings or to pump up kids in the middle of a serious meeting.

● Take Fun & Rowdy on a retreat or to a lock-in for hours of worship and entertainment!

● Involve your teenagers in church worship services with renditions of the songs and actions.

● Plan a whole meeting around each song, using its learning games and just-for-fun games. Teenagers will better understand the meaning of the song and will learn how the song relates to Scripture.

● Choose a game to play any time you need a fidget-buster to get kids up and moving! And you can play the song while kids play the game!

You'll love these upbeat songs and games and will be amazed at the enthusiasm you'll generate among your kids. And you'll really love this part: Preparation time is minimal for most games, and there's little or no expense involved!

Fun & Rowdy will get your teenagers praising God and learning Scripture while having a blast!

Ain't No Rock

Words and music by LaMarquis Jefferson. Copyright 1987 Integrity Praise Music. UBP

Ain't No Rock

Kids can stand either in rows or in a circle for this song. For all verses, have kids do a grapevine step: Step right foot to the side, then step left foot across in front, then step right foot to the side, then step left foot behind, and so forth. Step for eight counts to the right, then eight counts to the left, then eight to the right, then eight to the left, and so on. Add the motions if you'd like.

For the chorus, have kids stand in one place and stomp their feet to the beat as they do the motions.

1. **Ain't no rock gonna cry in my place.** *(Form a fist with right hand; hit the palm of left hand for eight counts.)*

As long as I'm alive, I'll glorify his holy name. *(Hold both hands overhead, and wave them side to side.)*

Ain't no rock gonna cry in my place. *(Form a fist with right hand; hit the palm of left hand for eight counts.)*

As long as I'm alive, I'll glorify his holy name. *(Hold both hands overhead, and wave them side to side.)*

Chorus:

Praise his holy name! *(Raise both hands high.)*

As long as I'm alive, I'll glorify his holy name. *(Wave hands side to side as you lower them to your sides.)*

Praise his holy name! *(Raise both hands high.)*

As long as I'm alive, I'll glorify his holy name. *(Wave hands side to side as you lower them to your sides.)*

2. **Ain't no tree gonna lift its branches.** *(Move both hands out to the side; then lift them high.)*

As long as I'm alive, I'll glorify his holy name. *(Wave hands side to side as you lower them.)*

Ain't no tree gonna lift its branches. *(Move both hands out to side; then lift them high.)*

As long as I'm alive, I'll glorify his holy name. *(Wave hands side to side as you lower them.)*

(Repeat chorus with actions.)

3. **Ain't no bird gonna sing in my place.** *(Move elbows at your side like wings.)*

As long as I'm alive, I'll glorify his holy name. *(Hold both hands overhead, and wave them side to side.)*

Ain't no bird gonna sing in my place. *(Move elbows at your side like wings.)*

As long as I'm alive, I'll glorify his holy name. *(Hold both hands overhead, and wave them side to side.)*

(Repeat chorus with actions.)

Barbershop Quartet

SUMMARY: In this **just-for-fun game**, teenagers will "shave" team members (with Popsicle sticks) while blindfolded.

PREPARATION: You'll need one Popsicle stick, a can of shaving cream, two blindfolds, a chair, a towel, and a bucket of water for each group of four people.

Have teenagers form groups of four. Assign one job to each person in each group: latherer, customer, shaver, and guide. In each group, drape the customer with a towel, and have him or her sit in the chair. Then blindfold the shaver and the latherer. Tell the groups that when you say "go," the guides are to verbally direct the latherers to lather the customers with shaving cream. When the customers are fully lathered, the guides are to verbally direct the shavers to shave off all the shaving cream with the Popsicle stick. The shaver may use the water to clean the stick. The first team to shave off all the shaving cream wins! If you have more time, have teenagers switch positions and play again!

Keep the Fire Going

SUMMARY: In this **learning game**, teenagers will try to pass a flame across a field without letting their opponents squirt out their flames.

PREPARATION: You'll need to play this game on an outdoor playing field. Supply a water-filled squirt gun for every fourth person and a small birthday candle for each person. You'll also need a table, a large candle, and either matches or lighters.

Set up the table at the middle of the far end of the playing field, stand the large candle on the table, and then give each person a small birthday candle. Have kids form teams of no more than ten. Have each team get in a line that stretches from one end of the field to the other, and position each team so its line is about five feet away from other teams. Assign one person in every four to be "squelchers," and give them water-filled squirt guns. Give the first person in each line a matchbook or lighter. To win the game, a team must use its birthday candles to pass a flame from the first person in its line, through the line, and to the large candle on the table while preventing other teams' squelchers from squirting out the flame. Players may move to dodge squelchers, but both players and squelchers must stay in line and in order across the field.

Say: **When I say "go," the first person in each line should light his or her own small candle. Then that person should light the candle of the next person in line. Continue passing the flame until the last person in line lights the large candle on the table. But be careful: There are squelchers on the other teams with squirt guns. If a squelcher puts out your team's flame, each person on your team must blow out his or her candle and start from the beginning. But squelchers must also light a candle to pass the flame. The first team to successfully light the big candle on the table wins!** Pause, make sure everyone understands, and then say: **Go!**

When the race is done, ask:

● **If the big candle represents God in our lives, how are the flames on our small candles in this race like our praises to God?**

● **What do the squelchers represent in our lives as Christians?**

● **How did you feel when you almost reached the big candle but then someone squelched your flame?**

● **How is this game like our efforts to praise and glorify God with a pure and sincere heart?**

I Believe

Word will— re-main to— the end.

I be-lieve I - sai- ah was a pro- phet of old.— The Lamb— was slain

just as he fore-told.— I— be-lieve Je - sus was the Word made man,

and he died for my sins, and he rose a- gain. Don't you know that I— be-lieve, I— be -

lieve, I— be - lieve in the Word of God.

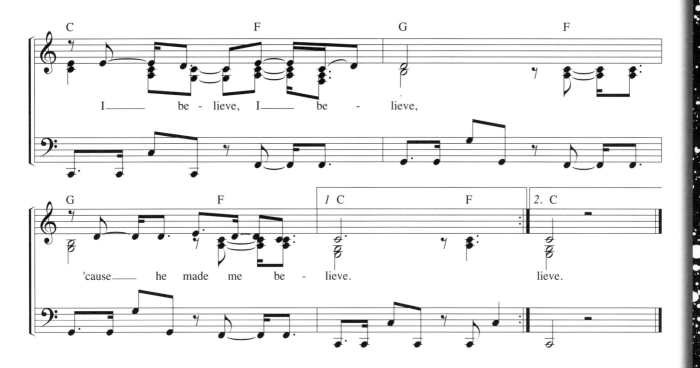

I_____ be - lieve, I_____ be - lieve,

'cause_____ he made me be - lieve.

lieve.

I Believe

Have kids form a circle, face left, and place their hands on the shoulders of the people in front of them. For the verses, have kids step to the beat of the music in this formation.

For the chorus, have kids dance freestyle to another spot in the circle, face left, and then place their hands on the shoulders of the person in front of them to get ready to sing the next verse.

For the coda, have kids form a circle and face the center. Choose one person to start by "giving five" to the person on his or her right. Then have that person give five to the person on his or her right, and so on until the "five" is passed around the circle.

VARIATIONS

● Each time kids take a new place in the circle, have them introduce themselves to the people on either side of them.

● Have kids give shoulder rubs each time they place their hands on the shoulders of the people in front of them.

● While everyone is doing the steps to the verses, have two or three volunteers get in the center of the circle and pantomime actions to the words.

● During the coda, which begins, "It's been passed down . . ." have kids do a quick "people pass." Have kids form two lines and face each other. Have one line of kids place their arms in front of them, cross their arms, and lock forearms with the people opposite them. Choose one person to be "passed down" the lines. Have that person stand at the head of the lines, cross his or her arms over his or her chest, lean back, and let the two lines pass him or her to the end and then gently set the person down.

Fold It and Fill It

SUMMARY: In this **learning game**, teenagers will create paper cups and will discover the importance of following God's instructions.

PREPARATION: You'll need a Bible, a pitcher of cool water, and an 8½-inch square of white paper for each person.

Give each person an 8½-inch square of paper. Say: **You all look thirsty! Let me come around and pour some water into your sheet of paper so you can have a drink.** Pour a few drops of water on a few sheets of paper. Then ask:

● **What was crazy about my statement?**

● **What went through your mind when I suggested that you drink from your papers?**

Say: **It may sound unbelievable, but you** *can* **drink from your sheet of paper. You just need to listen carefully and follow some special instructions.** Replace any wet papers, and lead kids through the following steps to make a paper cup.

1. Fold the paper in half diagonally so it creates an arrow that points up.

2. Fold the bottom right corner upward so it touches the middle of the left edge. Turn the paper over, and repeat this step.

3. Separate the top flaps, and fold the front flap into the front pocket. Fold the back flap into the back pocket. Open the center pocket to reveal a paper cup.

Pour some water into each person's cup. Ask:

● **How did my instructions help you get a drink?**

● **How valuable would these instructions be if you were very thirsty?**

Have a volunteer read Psalm 19:7-8. Ask:

● **How do God's instructions and commands in the Bible help us?**

● **When you trusted me and followed my instructions, you received a cool drink. What happens when we trust and obey God's Word?**

Say: **You couldn't get a drink without my special instructions. Without God's special instructions in the Bible, we can't drink in all the good news about Jesus. Just as this water is important for your health and refreshment, reading God's Word and following his commands are vital for spiritual health. When we follow God's Word, we drink living water!**

Pillowcase Catch

SUMMARY: In this **just-for-fun game**, teenagers will work in pairs to catch water balloons.

PREPARATION: You'll need an old pillowcase and four water balloons for every two kids in the group. Be sure kids are wearing bathing suits or clothes that can get wet.

Have teenagers form pairs. Then have partners form two lines, facing each other, about ten feet apart. Give a pillowcase to each player in line 1 and two water balloons to each player in line 2. Explain that the players in line 2 are the tossers and the players in line 1 are the catchers.

Say: **When I say "go," the tossers will toss their water balloons to the catchers, who will try to catch the balloons in their pillowcases. Since I know you're all up for a bigger challenge, the tossers will turn around so their backs are to the catchers.** Pause while the tossers turn around. Say: **Ready? Go!**

After the tossers have thrown their balloons, have partners trade roles and play again. If you have extra balloons, you may have a "toss off" between the pairs who caught the most balloons in their pillowcases.

I Have Decided

voice in - side kept tell - in' me   that I'd change by and by.___   But the
world be - gins to   see you change, don't ex - pect them   to ap - plaud.___   Just keep your

Spir - it made___ it   clear to me___   that   kind of life's___   a lie.   I have de -
eyes on him___   and   tell your - self,___   "I've be - come the work___   of God."

cid - ed___   I'm gon - na live___   like a be - liev - er, turn my back___   on the de - ceiv - er;   I'm gon - na

live what I   be - lieve.   I have de - cid - ed___   be - in' good___   is just a fa - ble;   I just can't

'cause I'm not a - ble.   I'm gon - na   leave it to   the Lord.___   So for -

I Have Decided

For the chorus, have kids do the parenthetical motions.

For the verses, have kids form two groups in the center of the room. Have each group form a line, one group facing one wall and the other group facing the opposite wall. Have both groups join hands and circle counterclockwise together throughout the verses. See illustration in margin.

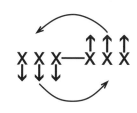

Chorus:

I have decided *(make a fist, and raise right arm from side to straight up in four counts)*
I'm gonna live like a believer *(make a fist, and raise left arm from side to straight up in four counts),*
Turn my back on the deceiver *(cross arms over chest, and step in an individual circle for four counts);*
I'm gonna live what I believe. *(Drop right arm down to right side; then drop left arm down to left side.)*
I have decided *(make a fist, and raise right arm straight up in four counts)*
Bein' good is just a fable *(make a fist, and raise left arm straight up in four counts);*
I just can't 'cause I'm not able. *(Cross arms over chest, and step in an individual circle for four counts.)*
I'm gonna leave it to the Lord. *(Drop right arm down to right side; then drop left arm down to left side.)*

VARIATIONS

● After the last "I'm gonna leave it to the Lord," have kids tell two other people how they'll live like a believer this next week.

● Have kids form three groups. Assign each group either verse 1, verse 2, or the chorus. Have each group come up with new actions to its assigned portion of the song and then teach the new song actions to each other.

● Instead of doing the large circle for the verses, have kids form one line and weave in and out of rows of chairs or pews.

Any Which Way You Can

SUMMARY: In this **just-for-fun game**, teenagers will try to score by using one of five different methods and pieces of sports equipment.

PREPARATION: You'll need an open area outside and a soccer ball, football, Frisbee, basketball, and softball or baseball. You'll also need two large trash cans for goals that you'll place at each end of the playing field.

Have kids form two equal teams, and have each team create a name. If you have an uneven number of people or a large group, rotate individuals throughout the game. Send teams out to the field, and have each team select a goalie to stand by a trash can. Begin the game by throwing the football up into the air with the instruction that kids can throw it, kick it, or run with it. After about a minute, throw in the soccer ball with the instruction that kids may only kick it. Then toss in the Frisbee, which they can only throw; the baseball, which they can only throw; and the basketball, which they must dribble while running and which they may pass.

At the end of ten minutes, the team with the most goals wins! You may wish to have a scorekeeper at each goal. If you notice that the game is getting too rough or that the guys aren't including the girls, you can take individuals out to sit in the "penalty box" for one-minute increments.

Magnetic Personality

SUMMARY: In this **learning game,** teenagers will discover how their commitment to Christ can affect others.

PREPARATION: You'll need eight boxes, eight small towels or pillowcases, a table, and four magnets that are powerful enough to pick up small items such as paper clips. In four of the boxes, place seventy-five to one hundred paper clips, tacks, nails, and staples—with each like item in a separate box. In the other four boxes, place a few things that a magnet won't be able to pick up, such as cereal, rubber bands, pencils, and paper wads.

Place the eight boxes on a table, and cover each with a towel or a pillowcase. Have kids form four teams, and give each team a magnet. Have the teams stand in single-file lines with their backs to the table, which should be about fifteen feet away. Say: **You don't know what's in each box, but some of the items will be attracted to your magnet, and some of the items will not. One at a time, you'll send a team member to the boxes. He or she will stick the magnet into any one of the eight boxes to see if the magnet picks anything up. If it does, that team member will take the items off, bring them back to your line, and begin a pile in front of your team. The rest of you will remain with your backs to the boxes so you won't be able to see in which box your team member searches. Continue the game like a relay, and at the end of five minutes, we'll count the items your team has collected. The team with the most items wins and will be named the team with the most magnetic personality!**

When the relay is finished, read John 15:5-8, and then ask:

● **How is the magnet's attraction to nails and paper clips like a Christian's commitment to Christ?**

● **How can you compare the nonmagnetized items to a noncommitted Christian?**

● **Just as the magnet controls the metal items, how do you give control to God when you commit to him?**

● **What guideline does the Bible give us regarding how we can bear fruit and therefore attract many non-Christians to Christ?**

Victory Chant

Hail, Je - sus, you're my king.

Hail, Je - sus, you're my king.

Your life frees me to sing.

Your life frees me to sing.

I will praise you all my days.

I will praise you all my days.

per - fect in all your ways.

You're per - fect in all your ways.

Hail, Je - sus, you're my Lord.

Hail, Je - sus, you're my Lord.

I will o - bey your Word.

I will o - bey your Word.

want to see your king-dom come.

I want to see your king-dom come.

Not my will but yours be done.

Not my will but yours be done.

Glo - ry, glo - ry to the Lamb.

Glo - ry, glo - ry to the Lamb.

You take me in - to the land.

You take me in - to the land.

We will con - quer in your name

We will con - quer in your name

and pro - claim that Je - sus reigns!

and pro - claim that Je - sus reigns!

23

Victory Chant

Have kids form two groups; have group 1 lead the motions and group 2 copy the motions.

1. **Hail, Jesus, you're my king.** *(Group 1 kids wave hands overhead and then side to side.)*
Hail, Jesus, you're my king. *(Group 2 kids wave hands overhead and then side to side.)*
Your life frees me to sing. *(Group 1 kids walk in individual circles.)*
Your life frees me to sing. *(Group 2 kids walk in individual circles.)*
I will praise you all my days. *(Group 1 kids wave hands overhead and then side to side.)*
I will praise you all my days. *(Group 2 kids wave hands overhead and then side to side.)*
You're perfect in all your ways. *(Group 1 kids walk in individual circles.)*
You're perfect in all your ways. *(Group 2 kids walk in individual circles.)*

2. **Hail, Jesus, you're my Lord.** *(Group 1 kids step right, bring feet together, step left, bring feet together.)*
Hail, Jesus, you're my Lord. *(Group 2 kids step right, bring feet together, step left, bring feet together.)*
I will obey your Word. *(Group 1 kids bend knees to the beat.)*
I will obey your Word. *(Group 2 kids bend knees to the beat.)*
I want to see your kingdom come. *(Group 1 kids step right, bring feet together, step left, bring feet together.)*
I want to see your kingdom come. *(Group 2 kids step right, bring feet together, step left, bring feet together.)*
Not my will but yours be done. *(Group 1 kids bend knees to the beat.)*
Not my will but yours be done. *(Group 2 kids bend knees to the beat.)*

(Repeat verse 1's actions for verse 3, and repeat verse 2's actions for verse 4.)

VARIATIONS

● Have group 1 kids think of their own actions, and have group 2 kids repeat the actions. Then switch so each group can think of its own actions.

● Have kids use furniture in the room for the movement to the song—for example, walk around a chair and tap on a table.

● Have kids form two lines. Have them face each other and join hands overhead so they form a long archway. Have kids walk two by two through the arch, making up actions as they go.

Build a Cheer

SUMMARY: In this **just-for-fun game**, teenagers will create cheers by adding one line per person.

PREPARATION: None.

Divide the group into teams of four, and spread the teams across the room. Have each team's members stand side by side, oldest to youngest, and assign a number to each team.

When everyone is in place, explain how the game Build a Cheer works. Say: **Each team will build a cheer, one line at a time, based on a topic selected by a different group. However, you won't know the topic until it's time for your team to perform.**

You'll have thirty seconds to secretly select a topic on which to build a

cheer. I'll then call out two numbers. The first will be the team to make up the cheer. The second number will be the team to assign the secret topic.

The first team will build its cheer based on that topic, with each person saying only one line. Once said, a line may not be changed, and team members may not repeat previous lines.

Here's the catch: After a topic is assigned, I will say "oldest" or "youngest" to refer to the person who is to start the cheer. This way, no one will know who will start or finish.

Have the teams select topics and begin building their cheers. You may want to award prizes for the funniest and best-rhyming cheers or for the cheer built in the shortest amount of time. One alternative to this game is to build new cheers and add motions to each line.

Jump a Dollar

SUMMARY: In this **learning game,** teenagers will try to jump over a dollar bill while holding their toes to learn about praise in the face of defeat.

PREPARATION: You'll need a Bible, dollar bills, and someone to be a "positive" player. Secretly tell this person to be completely positive in cheering others on by saying such things as "You're great!" or "I believe in you!" and "You can do it!"

To explain the game and to demonstrate the position kids are to take, say: **With your feet together, bend over, grab your toes, and jump over this dollar bill without letting go of your toes. Both feet must completely clear the dollar bill. The first person to successfully jump over the dollar bill wins and gets to keep it.**

Have the group form a single-file line on one side of the dollar bill, with the positive player near the front. Let everyone take turns jumping. The positive player will also take a turn jumping and should praise each person after he or she jumps even if he or she is unsuccessful.

Play until everyone has jumped, and award dollar bills to all of the winners. Don't be surprised if no one wins; this activity is a real challenge. Then ask:

● **How did it feel to lose when you had such a short distance to jump? For the winners, how did it feel to win?**

● **Were you ever tempted to bend the rules? Why or why not?**

● **In what ways did the person with the positive attitude affect your perspective during the game?**

Read aloud Philippians 4:8-9 and 1 Peter 4:11; then ask:

● **What happens when we find good things to say? What happens when we dwell on bad things?**

● **What can we do this week to speak words of praise to families? friends? those outside our group?**

Lean on Me

call on your bro - ther when you need a hand; we all need some - bo - dy to le - - - an on. I just might have a pro - blem that you'll un - der - stand; we all need some - bo - dy to le - - an on. Lean on me an on.

Lean on Me

For the chorus, have kids drape their arms over each other's shoulders and lean side to side.

For the verses, have kids clap to the beat up over their left shoulder while they place their right foot out to the side and then clap next to their right hip while they place their left foot out to the side.

Chorus:
Lean on me when you're not strong,
And I'll be your friend, and I'll help you carry on.
For it won't be long
'Til I'm gonna need somebody to lean on.

1. You just call   on   your   brother   when you need   a   hand;

We all need   somebody   to   lean   on.

I just might   have   a   problem   that you'll understand;

We all need   somebody   to   lean   on.

(Repeat chorus and verse with actions.)

VARIATIONS

● During the chorus, have each person find a partner. Have each pair stand back to back, hook elbows, try to sit all the way down to the ground, and try to then stand up—never letting loose of each other.

● Have everyone form a circle and hold hands. Have all kids lean back as far as they can without breaking the circle and with everyone holding hands to support people on either side.

Balloon Backup

SUMMARY: In this **just-for-fun game**, teenagers will try to gather and carry balloons while linked back to back.

PREPARATION: You'll need six chairs and sixty uninflated balloons (ten each of six different colors). Set four chairs in each corner of the room, and set two back to back in the middle of the room. Separate the balloons by color, keeping them uninflated, and place ten balloons of the same color on each chair.

Separate your group into pairs, and direct their attention to the six chairs and piles of balloons. Explain that partners will be competing to see which pair can gather the most balloons before time runs out.

Say: **The object of this game is to pick up, inflate, and carry as many balloons as you can with your partner. You'll move to a chair, pick up one balloon, inflate it, and tie it off at that chair. You may then pick up a balloon of a different color from a different chair. However, no pair may approach a chair where other players are working at that time. The first pair to reach a chair is the first to get a balloon. Furthermore, each pair must have one balloon of each color before starting over with the same colors.**

Here's the catch: Standing back to back, you'll lock arms and carry the inflated balloons between yourselves while moving across the floor. If a balloon falls along the way, you may try and get it back, but you can't unlock your arms to do so.

Other pairs may try to pop the balloons you drop on the floor before you can pick them up. However, no one can intentionally cause any pair to drop its balloons.

Allow five minutes for the pairs to play, and then declare a winner.

Huff and Puff

SUMMARY: In this **learning game**, teenagers will use their breath to balance a sheet of paper, showing how one can endure with teamwork.

PREPARATION: You'll need a Bible, table, chairs, and one sheet of 8½-by-11-inch paper for every two people.

Have kids form pairs, and have each person sit at the table across from his or her partner. Players should lean inward so that their faces are approximately twelve inches away from their partners' faces. Kids can use their arms and elbows for support.

After everyone is in place, give each pair a sheet of paper. Say: **Stand the paper on its side halfway between you and your partner. When I say "go," release the paper. You and your partner will try to keep the paper standing by using only your breath. Once play has begun, at no time may your hands or anything else be used to keep the paper up.**

When your paper falls flat, you and your partner must lean back in your chairs and whistle "Lean on Me" until everyone else has finished. The goal is to see which pair can keep its paper standing upright the longest.

Play several rounds, then ask:

● What was the most frustrating part of this activity? Why?

● What was most rewarding? Why?

● Did you and your partner develop a strategy to keep the paper standing upright? If so, what was it?

● How was it to keep going while others were whistling?

● Did you find yourselves encouraging each other during the game? If so, how did it feel to give or receive such encouragement?

● What does this say about working together?

Read aloud Romans 15:1-7. Ask:

● What can we do this week to encourage and help bring balance to our families? friends? others in our community?

King of the Jungle

Well the day has just be-gun, and I'm al-read-
say this world's a jun-gle, and some-times

y run-nin' late, with too man-y ir-ons in the fire and too
I must ad-mit I'd be scared to death if I did not know who

much on my plate. I'd be pull-in' out my hair if I could just
was king of it. But the truth is, God cre-at-ed this whole world

get one hand free, and I'd stop this world if I could find the key!
with his own hand, so ev-ery-thing is un-der his com-mand.

Go To Chorus

And

30

praise   you!   Lord,   we   praise _____   you!

You   are _____   the   King   of   kings!   (Lord   we)

King of the Jungle

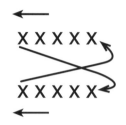

For the verses, have kids form two groups. Then have groups form single-file, parallel lines about ten feet apart, with everyone facing the same direction. Have kids walk forward with their lines toward the wall. Then have the first person in each line cross diagonally to the back of the other line. (See diagram in the margin.) When those two people cross in the center, have them clap hands. Have kids continue this pattern, with the first person in each line crossing diagonally to the back of the other line and clapping hands as they cross.

Have kids follow the parenthetical motions for the chorus.

For the bridge, have groups alternate singing lines and stepping in place to the beat.

Chorus:

What I feel is tellin' me I'm goin' crazy *(step in place, right, left, right, left; then hold hands to head)*,
But what is real says God's still on his throne. *(Step in place, right, left, right, left; then motion wide with arms out to sides.)*
What I need is to remember one thing *(step in place, right, left, right, left; then hold up one finger)*:
That the Lord of the gentle breeze *(raise both arms overhead, and turn in individual circles)*
Is Lord of the rough and tumble *(roll arms in front)*,
And he is the King of the jungle. *(Turn to join hands, and send a "wave" down the line, starting with the first person in line.)*
Yes, he is! *(Send the wave back to the left.)*

Creation Creators

SUMMARY: In this **learning game,** teenagers will create objects out of modeling dough and will compare that activity to God's sovereignty.

PREPARATION: For every three kids, you'll need a handful of modeling dough or clay. You'll also need a pencil and a sheet of paper. For best results, play this game on a floor without carpet.

Have kids sit on the floor in groups of three. Give each group a handful of clay or modeling dough.

Say: **We're going to play the game Creation Creators. But before we begin, I want you all to think of things that God created and shout your ideas out loud. For example, you might choose flowers, people, dogs, trees, or rainbows.**

As the teenagers begin to shout out their ideas, write them down on the piece of paper. Continue writing until you have about twenty items.

Say: **When I name an object, each group is to create it out of the modeling dough. For example, if I say "stars," everyone in your group has to help make a star with the modeling dough. The first group to make the object that most resembles what I said wins a point. At the end of the game, whoever has the most points wins.**

Play several rounds. Then ask:

● **Was it difficult to have three people trying to make something with a little bit of modeling dough? Why or why not?**

Have each group divide its modeling dough into three equal pieces. Play a few more rounds, with each person using his or her own piece of dough. Then ask:

● **In which situation did you have the most control over the end result: as a group or by yourself?**

● **Can two or more people be equally in control of something at the same time?**

Say: **You are like modeling dough in God's hands. He wants to shape and form you to be more like Jesus through challenging situations and circumstances. During these times you have two choices. You can either face them with your own strength, trying to control the people and circumstances around you, or you can trust in the One who created you by giving him total control of everything. When you feel like you can't handle life and think that things are out of control, remember that God created the whole world, which means there's nothing too big for him to handle.**

Jungle Gibberish

SUMMARY: In this **just-for-fun game,** kids will ask one another to act like jungle animals.

PREPARATION: You'll need to make a list of jungle animals and their behaviors along with some extra descriptive details. Your list may look like this:

Have someone with long hair roar like a lion.

Have someone wearing a colorful shirt squawk like a bird.

Have someone wearing glasses laugh like a hyena.

Have someone with brown eyes slither like a snake.

Have someone wearing black shoes act like a monkey.

Have someone wearing pink grunt like a wild pig.

For each person, you'll need a copy of the list and a pencil. You'll also need a box of animal cookies.

Give each teenager a copy of the list and a pencil. Then say: **This room is going to turn into a jungle. On the count of three, you need to find people who fit the jungle-animal descriptions on the list to act like that jungle animal. For example, ask someone wearing black shoes to act like a monkey. When that person is finished acting out the role, have him or her initial your list next to that description. The person who has his or her list completed first wins the game.**

Give the winner the box of animal cookies.

Big House

we can play foot-ball, a big, big house.

it's my Fa-ther's house!   house.

it's my Fa-ther's house!   It's a big, big

house, it's my Fa-ther's house!

D.C. first time

Big House

Have kids form two lines about five feet apart; then have the lines face each other. Have kids spread out so each person has some room on both sides.

For the verses, have kids walk forward for eight counts to walk between two people in the opposite line. Then have kids turn around and walk eight counts back to their original line. They can repeat this motion throughout the verses.

For the chorus, have kids stay in their lines to do the parenthetical motions.

Chorus:

Come and go with me *(motion, "Come here")*

To my Father's house. *(Hold up both arms; then shake arms in the air.)*

Come and go with me *(motion, "Come here")*

To my Father's house. *(Hold up both arms; then shake arms in the air.)*

It's a big, big house *(make the "roof" of a "house" with hands close together in front; then move them wider apart, then wider)*

With lots and lots of rooms *(turn in individual circles)*,

A big, big table *(make the sides of a "table" with hands close together in front; then move them wider apart, then wider)*

With lots and lots of food. *(Turn in individual circles.)*

It's a big, big yard *(hold hands close together in front; then move them wider apart, then wider)*

Where we can play football *(pretend to toss a football)*,

A big, big house. *(Hold hands close together in front; then move them wider apart, then wider.)*

It's my Father's house! *(Hold up both arms, then shake arms in the air.)*

Blueprint Bingo

SUMMARY: In this **learning game**, students will race to correctly complete the blueprint of a functional dream house.

PREPARATION: You'll need to make five copies on poster board of a house "blueprint" that includes a kitchen, living room, dining room, bedrooms, bathrooms, garage, and yard. Be sure to indicate on the blueprints what the rooms are. You'll also need to think of a list of twenty to thirty items that you might find in a house and write each item on four small pieces of paper. The list might include a credenza, ottoman, chandelier, rocking chair, changing table, armoire, chesterfield, daybed, and bidet, among others. Include some items that are less familiar. After you've created four identical lists of items, place each complete list in a paper lunch bag. Next create a master blueprint by writing the name of each item in its correct room on one of the poster board blueprints. The master blueprint will serve as the model that the kids will try to match. You'll also need a Bible.

Have the kids line up in four teams. Place a poster board blueprint and a paper lunch bag of listed items on the opposite side of the room from each team. Have members from each team take turns running to their blueprint, pulling out a piece of paper from the lunch bag, and determining where on the blueprint the item belongs. Each team member can either move the previous piece or select a new one. When the team has placed all the pieces and believes the blueprint is correct, the team must call you over to compare its house to the model. If the team's blueprint is wrong, don't tell them which pieces are wrong; just tell them that they need to do more work. The first team to create a blueprint that matches the master blueprint wins!

When the game is over, read John 14:1-6, and then ask:
- **What would your dream house include?**
- **What do you think Jesus meant when he said, "There are many rooms in my Father's house"?**
- **In what ways will our heavenly mansions be different from the ones we build here on earth?**

Life Savers Limbo

SUMMARY: In this **just-for-fun game**, teenagers will dig through rice to find their teams' colors.

PREPARATION: You'll need twelve rolls of five-flavor Life Savers candies, a child's plastic wading pool (or other similar plastic container), four clear cups, and five two-pound bags of rice. Pour the rice into the wading pool. Then, keeping one roll of Life Savers as a prize, hide all the other Life Savers candies except the green ones in the rice. Finally, hide three green Life Savers candies in the pool. (Note: You can wash and reuse the rice later, or you can use Styrofoam peanuts instead.)

Have kids form four teams, give each team one clear cup, and assign each team one of four flavors: lemon, pineapple, cherry, and orange. Tell the teams that everyone on each team will have a turn to dig through the rice and try to find his or her team's assigned flavor. Have each team line up and prepare to send one person at a time to the pool.

Say: **When it's your turn, you may take one two-handed scoop of rice. If you find your team's flavor of Life Savers, put the candies in your team cup. But here's the catch. If you scoop up a green Life Savers candy, you have to pour back all the Life Savers in your cup. At the end of five minutes, the team with the most Life Savers wins!** After the game, give a roll of Life Savers candies to the winning team.

Do, Lord

45

Do, Lord

Have teenagers form three groups to sing and clap to the song in a unique way. Repeat the parenthetical motions for the verses and the chorus.

1. **I've got a home** *(group 1 claps hands overhead)* **in gloryland** *(group 2 joins in with group 1 and all clap their hands overhead)*
That outshines the sun. *(Group 3 joins in and claps hands overhead.)*
I've got a home *(group 1 continues clapping but brings hands down)* **in gloryland** *(group 2 joins group 1 and claps with hands down)*
That outshines the sun. *(Group 3 joins in and claps with hands down.)*
I've got a home *(group 1 claps hands overhead)* **in gloryland** *(group 2 joins in and claps hands overhead)*
That outshines the sun *(group 3 joins in and claps hands overhead),*
'Way beyond the blue. *(All groups clap once as loud as they can on the word " 'way," then move hands in a circle, then continue clapping on the word "blue.")*

Chorus:

Do, Lord *(group 1),* **oh do, Lord** *(group 2),*
Oh do remember me *(group 3).*
Do, Lord *(group 1),* **oh do, Lord** *(group 2),*
Oh do remember me *(group 3).*
Do, Lord *(group 1),* **oh do, Lord** *(group 2),*
Oh do remember me *(group 3),*
(With verse 1) 'Way beyond the blue. *(All groups.)*
(With verse 2) While he's calling you. *(All groups.)*

VARIATIONS

● During the chorus, have partners hook right arms and circle, then hook left arms and circle.

● Have kids sing verse 2 while lining up one at a time as if they're joining in and following a leader.

Goin' for the Gloryland

SUMMARY: In this **just-for-fun game**, teenagers will have a blast learning more about cooperation and teamwork with just a bundle of plastic grocery bags.

PREPARATION: You'll need a used plastic grocery bag for each teenager and a large, open space either outside or in a large class-room with furniture pushed out of the way.

Have teenagers form two teams. The larger the teams, the better. Have teams stand on opposite sides of the room, and have team members stand shoulder to shoulder, facing the other team. Give each person a plastic grocery bag.

When everyone has a plastic grocery bag in his or her hand, say: **The first two people on this team** (designate the starting team) **will begin our "Goin' for the Gloryland" relay by tying their ankles together with one bag as if in a three-legged race. These two will race over to the other team and will tie** another person's ankle to one of their ankles. Continue running back and forth, adding a new team member each time by tying his or her ankle to the ankle of one of the end team members. After you've finished, everyone in this room will be tied together at the ankles. Then "go to the gloryland" by dancing together across the room.

Jesus Slogans

SUMMARY: In this **learning game**, teenagers will remember to put Jesus first in their lives by creating slogans using common items.

PREPARATION: You'll need a Bible for each person and a box containing common items such as a candle, a ball, a pencil, scissors, paper, a cup, or a leaf. Include more items than there are kids.

Have teenagers sit in a large circle. Make sure you have enough items in the box for each person to remember a different item.

Say: **I'll show each of you the items in this box. You'll each get about five seconds to look carefully at all of the items in the box.** Go around the circle and show the box to each teenager. At this point you may want to have the group sing the song "Do, Lord" to allow some time to lapse before going into the next part of the game.

Then say: **Try and remember one or two items in the box. As we go around the circle, make up a slogan about Jesus using one of the items. For example, for a pair of scissors someone might say, "Jesus is like a pair of scissors because he helps me cut out sin in my life" or "Jesus is like a piece of paper because he gives me a clean sheet each day."** As each item is named, pull it out of the box. If someone can't remember an item that's left in the box when it's his or her turn, let that person use an item already that's already been named to create a slogan. After each teenager has had a chance to make up a slogan with which to remember Jesus, ask:

● **Why are slogans effective advertising tools?**

● **What are some slogans from products we use every day?**

● **During what specific time this week can you use one of the slogans you created to advertise for Jesus?**

Say: **Just as advertising slogans remind us of certain products, slogans can help us remember Jesus—and he always remembers us. Let's read some of the "Jesus slogans" in the Bible.** Read these Scriptures together: John 4:13-14; 6:35; 8:12; 10:9; 10:11; and 14:6.

Love Jive

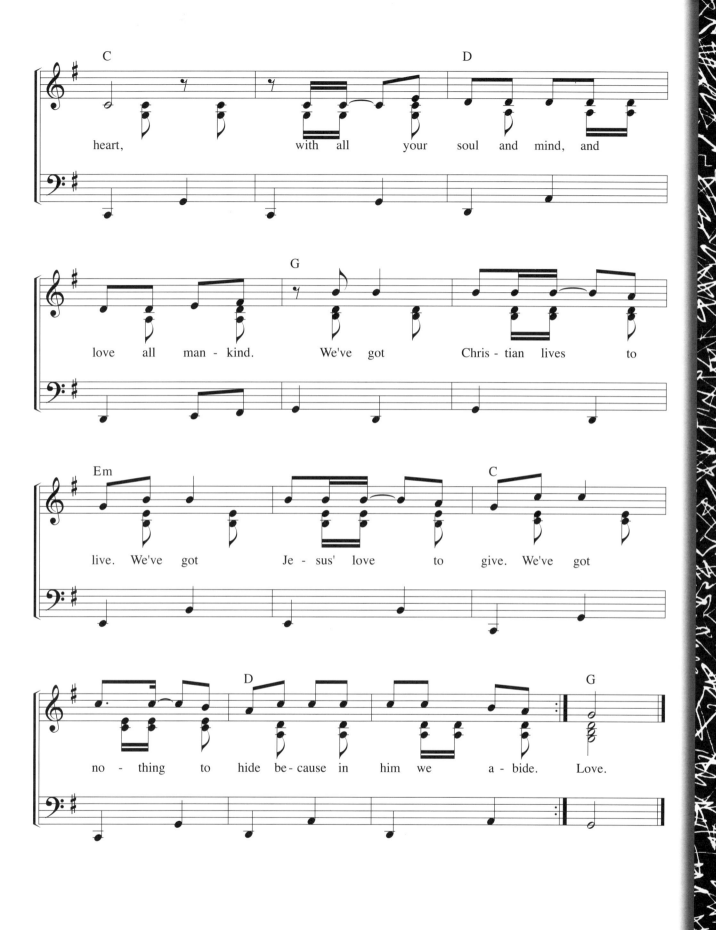

49

Love Jive

Have kids do the "hand jive" for this song. Here's how to do it: Pat your thighs twice; clap twice; with your palms flat and facing the ground, cross your right hand over your left twice; with your hands in same position, cross your left hand over your right hand twice; make a "hitchhiker motion" with your right thumb over your right shoulder twice; make the same motion with your left thumb over your left shoulder twice. Repeat the hand jive throughout the song.

VARIATIONS

● Have kids get into pairs to sing the song and switch partners each time they repeat it.

● In their pairs, have kids tell their partners one way to show they love God with their hearts.

● Make up a variety of questions that have to do with the song's lyrics. Then have kids switch partners each time they sing the song. Ask a question, and have kids give a quick response to their partner. For example, ask "How do you love others as you would yourself?" or "What's hard about living a Christian life?"

Just Do It ... All!

SUMMARY: In this **learning game**, teenagers will explore how distractions in our lives make it hard to focus on our love for God.

PREPARATION: You'll need sheets of newsprint, tape, and markers.

Have kids form four groups, and have the groups line up at one end of the room. Tape a sheet of newsprint to a wall directly across from each group, and place several markers at each sheet of newsprint.

Say: **I want to find out what things are most important to you. This relay will help me find out very quickly. When I say "go," the first person in each line will run to the paper across from his or her line and pick up a marker in each hand. Then each player will draw the two things that are most important to him or her. But you'll have to draw them both at the same time. So that I can learn even more about you, while you're drawing I want you to recite your Social Security number, phone number, address, and tell me what school you go to. When you've drawn your pictures, put down the markers, and tag the next person in your line. Ready? Go!**

After the kids have completed their drawings, take the newsprint off the wall, and have each group form a circle around their sheet. Ask:

● **What can you learn from these drawings?**
● **Why aren't these helpful in learning about what's important to you?**
● **What would have been a better way to find out?**

Say: **These papers reflect the things that are important to us.** Ask:

● **How does your life reflect the things that are most important to you?**

Say: **In this relay, you had to focus on too many things at once. That made it impossible for you to really show me the important things in your life.** Ask:

● **What things make it hard to show God how much we love him?**
● **How can you show God—not tell him—how important he is to you?**

Turn over the sheets of paper, and distribute markers. Have kids work together to make a "Love Jive" card, expressing their love for God.

Ring-a-Thing Golf

SUMMARY: In this **just-for-fun game**, teenagers will attempt to ring items with a Hula Hoop.

PREPARATION: You'll need pencils and several Hula Hoops. If your church doesn't have a children's play area, make arrangements to car pool to a local park that has a wide variety of playground equipment. List about ten "ringable" items that you see in the children's play area on a sheet of paper; then photocopy the list for your players. You might list items such as a drinking fountain, a tree branch, a teeter-totter, a picnic basket, or someone on a swing.

Gather teenagers near a children's play area, and have them form groups of no more than four. Give each group a Hula Hoop, a pencil, and a photocopy of the list of items to ring.

Explain that groups will have twenty minutes to use a Hula Hoop to ring each item on the list. Keeping score is similar to that in golf; each attempt receives one point until the item is "rung," and players must rotate taking turns. Players must stand at least twenty feet from the targets. After twenty minutes, gather groups, and have kids tally their team scores. Congratulate the team with the lowest score. You might include prizes such as Hula Hoops or gift certificates to a miniature golf center.

Overflowing Fun!

SUMMARY: In this **just-for-fun game**, teenagers will work in teams to transport cups of water across a playing area.

PREPARATION: You'll need water; four or six plastic cups; two large, plastic trash cans; two buckets; an outdoor playing area; and two pingpong balls. Let kids know in advance to wear bathing suits or clothes that can get wet. Before kids arrive, fill the trash cans with water, and place them at one end of the playing area. Set two empty buckets at the opposite end, and drop a pingpong ball into each bucket.

Have kids form two teams, and have each team line up between its empty bucket and its full container. Give each team two or three plastic cups. Say: **In this game, your team will transport the water in your trash can to the empty bucket at the other end of the playing area. You'll need to put enough water in the bucket to spill the ball out of the bucket. Pass the full cups down the line, pour the water in the bucket, and pass the "empties" back as quickly as possible. Ready? Go!**

Congratulate the team that fills its bucket first. For a fun variation, your group could try this game tossing water balloons instead of passing cups of water; to play this way, have the person standing closest to the bucket break the balloon into the bucket.

I Got the Want To

I Got the Want To

Have kids form two concentric circles—circle 1 and circle A—with an equal number of people in each circle. In every part of the song but the chorus, have circle 1 walk clockwise and circle A walk counterclockwise.

For the chorus, have circles 1 and A face each other so everyone has a partner. If there are an uneven number of kids, have them form one trio, too. Have kids find new partners each time they repeat the chorus.

If you don't have a willing soloist, have circle 1 sing the "solo" part and circle A sing "all."

SOLO: **Walk in the light as he is in the light.** *(Circle 1 walks clockwise to the beat.)*

ALL: **Walkin', a-walkin'.** *(Circle A walks counterclockwise two steps, moving to the beat—one step on "walkin'" and the second step on "a-walkin'.")*

SOLO: **Walk in the light as he is in the light.** *(Circle 1 walks clockwise.)*

ALL: **Walkin', a-walkin'.** *(Circle A walks counterclockwise two steps.)*

SOLO: **Walk in the light as he is in the light.** *(Circle 1 walks clockwise.)*

ALL: **Walkin', a-walkin'.** *(Circle A walks counterclockwise two steps.)*

SOLO: **Walk in the light as he is in the light.** *(Circle 1 walks clockwise.)*

ALL: **Walkin', a-walkin'.** *(Circle A walks counterclockwise two steps.)*

Chorus:

SOLO: **I got the want to.** *(Circle 1 raises right arms.)*

ALL: **I got the want to.** *(Circle A raises left arms to mirror circle 1's actions.)*

SOLO: **I got the need to.** *(Circle 1 raises left arms.)*

ALL: **I got the need to.** *(Circle A raises right arms to mirror circle 1's actions.)*

SOLO: **I need to follow through.** *(Circle 1 puts arms down.)*

ALL: **I need to follow through.** *(Circle A puts arms down.)*

SOLO: **That's why I need you** *(circle 1 points with right fingers),*

ALL: **Need you** *(circle A points with left fingers),*

SOLO: **I need you** *(circle 1 points with left fingers),*

ALL: **Need you.** *(Circle A points with right fingers.)*

VARIATIONS

● Get a flashlight, and shine it on one person. Have the other kids shout out ways they see that person walking in the light or showing Jesus' love to others. Be sure to shine the spotlight on every person.

Shaky, Breaky Hearts!

SUMMARY: In this **learning game**, teenagers will share handshakes and hearts to show the importance of continually giving away God's love.

PREPARATION: You'll need a Bible and a pink, five-inch, construction paper heart for every person.

Give each person a paper heart, and ask kids to tear their hearts into the same number of pieces as there are people in the group.

Explain that each person will give away all of his or her heart pieces, one at a time. In order to give away a heart piece, a person must also give two hand-shakes by crossing one arm over the other. Failure to do so will result in giving two heart pieces instead of one. No one may give heart pieces to the same person more than once per visit. Everyone must accept a heart piece whenever approached. The recipients must take the heart piece, look the giver in the eye and say, "Thank you" before moving on.

Allow two minutes for kids to play the game. After two minutes, ask if any-one has managed to end the game without any heart pieces. Chances are that everyone will have several pieces. Ask:

● **Which was easier—sharing heart pieces and handshakes or saying, "Thank you"? Why?**

● **What made it more difficult?**

● **Would it have been possible to give away all your heart pieces?**

● **How did it feel to know that for every heart piece you gave away, you continued to get more?**

Have several volunteers read aloud Psalm 118:1-4; John 13:34-35; and Romans 13:8-10. Then ask:

● **What do these verses say about the love of God?**

● **What do they say about our responsibility to those around us?**

● **How can we demonstrate an unending and sincerely Christlike love for others this week?**

Speed Echo

SUMMARY: In this **just-for-fun game**, teenagers will echo motions and sound effects as fast as possible.

PREPARATION: You'll need two prizes for the winners of this game.

Have teenagers stand in a circle. When everyone is in place, explain how Speed Echo works.

Say: **I'll make a simple motion and sound effect, such as tugging my left ear and saying "boo!" The person to my right must repeat both as fast as possible. Each person in the circle will repeat both as fast as possible until they reach the starting point again.**

At that point, the person to my right will perform the original motion and sound and will then add one of his or her own to be repeated around the circle.

Each person will have a chance to add a motion and a sound, but before something may be added, all previous motions and sounds must be performed.

If a person forgets something along the way, he or she is out of the game. Players are eliminated until there are only two left. The two finalists will have a runoff, with each person adding motions and sounds until someone misses and one is declared the winner.

Award a sound effects cassette or compact disc to the winner and a small speed-reading book to the runner-up.

What We've Come Here For

Love is— what we've— come here for;— this is why— we're stay-
Truth is— what we've— come here for;— this is why— we're stay-

in'.— Love is— what we've— come here for,— the
in'.— Truth is— what we've— come here for,— the

kind that won't— be fad - in'.— The kind that stands and—
kind that won't— be fad - in'.— The kind of truth that can

knocks at my heart, the kind that's loved— me from the start.—
set a man free, the kind I want— my heart to see.—

Love is why we've come.   Love has a name:
Truth is why we've come.   Truth has a name:

What We've Come Here For

Have kids follow the parenthetical motions.

1. Love is what we've come here for *(cross arms over chest; then spread arms out to sides)*;
This is why we're stayin'. *(Point to the ground.)*
Love is what we've come here for *(cross arms over chest; then spread arms out to sides)*,
The kind that won't be fadin'. *(Shake index finger.)*
The kind that stands and knocks at my heart *(pretend to knock; then cross arms over chest)*,
The kind that's loved me from the start. *(Spread arms out.)*
Love is why we've come. *(Cross arms over chest, then march in place.)*

Chorus:

Love has a name: Jesus. *(Cross arms over chest; then point straight up.)*
Love has a name: Jesus. *(Cross arms over chest; then point straight up.)*
Love has a name. *(Cross arms over chest.)*

2. Truth is what we've come here for *(point to mouth; then spread arms out to sides)*;
This is why we're stayin'. *(Point to the ground.)*
Truth is what we've come here for *(point to mouth; then spread arms out to sides)*,
The kind that won't be fadin'. *(Shake index finger.)*
The kind of truth that can set a man free *(spread arms wide)*,
The kind I want my heart to see. *(Cross arms over chest.)*
Truth is why we've come. *(Point to mouth; then march in place.)*

Chorus (revised):

Truth has a name: Jesus. *(Point to mouth; then point straight up.)*
Truth has a name: Jesus. *(Point to mouth; then point straight up.)*
Truth has a name. *(Point to mouth.)*

3. Hope is what we've come here for *(raise both arms up; then spread arms out to sides)*;
This is why we're stayin'. *(Point to the ground.)*
Hope is what we've come here for *(raise both arms up; then spread arms out to sides)*;
The kind that won't be fadin'. *(Shake index finger.)*
The kind that gives me a reason to live *(spread arms wide)*,
The kind that only God can give. *(Point straight up.)*
Hope is why we've come. *(Raise both arms up; then march in place.)*

Chorus (revised):

Hope has a name: Jesus. *(Raise both arms up; then point up with one finger.)*
Hope has a name: Jesus. *(Raise both arms up; then point up with one finger.)*
Truth has a name: Jesus. *(Point to mouth; then point straight up.)*
Truth has a name: Jesus. *(Point to mouth; then point straight up.)*
Love has a name: Jesus. *(Cross arms over chest; then point straight up.)*
Love has a name: Jesus. *(Cross arms over chest; then point straight up.)*
Jesus. *(Cross arms over chest.)*

Ramblin' Roads

SUMMARY: In this **just-for-fun game,** teenagers will move back and forth across a room while their teammates run in circles around them.

PREPARATION: You'll need a whistle and prizes.

Gather the group at one end of a room, and have kids form teams of three. Separate each team in approximately three-foot increments.

Say: **Your team's goal is to move back and forth across the room as quickly as possible. Two players will lock arms, stand back to back, and move together; the third person will run clockwise around them. Choose who will be your first, second, and third runners.**

The running player will tell the others on the team things he or she loves, such as ice cream, puppies, Jesus, football, and so on.

When you hear the whistle, the next player will begin running in a circle while the first runner locks arms with the third team member. Play will resume with the new runner sharing things he or she loves. When the whistle blows again, the third member will repeat this sequence.

Tell the kids that they'll also play two other rounds, using the whistle as the signal to change rounds. In the second round, they'll share things they find true; in the third, things they hope for.

After you've explained how the game works, say: **Before returning to the starting end of the room, your entire team must touch the opposite wall and yell as loudly as possible. Then get to the starting wall, touch it, quickly sit on the floor, and yell again.**

Play the game, blowing the whistle faster and faster each time. Declare one team the winner, and award a prize such as "Baby (T)Ruth" candy bars.

The Really Relay

SUMMARY: In this **just-for-fun game,** teenagers will pull items from a bag and will share facts and opinions about the items.

PREPARATION: You'll need a paper bag and one common household item per person, such as a comb, a sponge, or a rubber band. Put the items in the bag, and close it.

Ask the group to sit in a circle while you explain how the Really Relay works. Hold up the paper bag that contains an item for each person.

Say: **Without looking inside the bag, our first player will pull one object from the bag and will give the item to the person on his or her left. This person will share one fact about the object, using the word "really."** For example, you could say, "This comb is *really* plastic."

That player will then pull another object from the bag and will hand it to the next person to the left, who will then share a "really" fact about the object. Each object will stay with its "owner" until the next round. The last player will give the final object to the first player. Then we'll pass the bag around and return the objects.

We'll play two more rounds. On the second round, tell something you really love about your item. On the third round, share a silly reason why you hope to get the item at Christmas—still using the word "really."

Play until everyone has shared in each round.

Crown Him With Many Crowns

Crown Him With Many Crowns

Have kids stand in one large circle to sing verse 1. For verse 2, have kids form two circles and repeat the actions within their new circles. Then have kids form three circles for verse 3 and four circles for verse 4. It's OK if only two or three kids are in each circle.

1. **Crown him with many crowns** *(walk forward to the center of the circle for eight counts, raising arms high)*,

The Lamb upon his throne *(walk backward for eight counts, bringing arms down)*;

Hark! How the heav'nly anthem drowns *(walk to the right for four counts and then to the left for four counts)*

All music but its own! *(Walk to the right for four counts and then to the left for four counts.)*

Awake, my soul, and sing *(walk forward to the center for eight counts, raising arms high)*

Of him who died for thee *(walk backward for eight counts, bringing arms down)*,

And hail him as thy matchless King *(walk to the right for four counts and then to the left for four counts)*

Through all eternity. *(Walk to the right for four counts and then to the left for four counts.)*

Words by Matthew Bridges and Godfrey Thring. Music by George J. Elvey.

VARIATIONS

● Have kids perform this song for the congregation as a worship dance. Give each teenager a three-foot red streamer for each hand. When kids step to the right for four counts and to the left for four counts, have them hold their streamers high.

Crown of Jewels

SUMMARY: In this **learning game**, teenagers will learn that they can become jewels in Jesus' kingly crown by being more like him.

PREPARATION: For each group of five, you'll need fifteen to twenty empty pop cans, eight pieces of scrap paper or newspaper, a blank piece of paper, a pencil, and a five-foot-diameter masking tape "crown" circle on the floor. You'll also need a Bible. Randomly space the crown circles throughout the room, and place the cans, newspaper, paper, and pencil in each circle.

Have kids form teams of five. Say: **In this game, each group will try to build a "kingly crown" by stacking pop cans inside their circle.** Ask each group to designate a "recorder."

Say: **Each of the pop cans in your pile represents a jewel that only you can place in the crown of Jesus, the king. Always staying inside your crown circle, stack the cans on top of each other and try to keep your crown intact. As you stack each can, say aloud one "jewel"—or attribute or quality—of Jesus, the King. Your recorder will write down each jewel you place in Jesus' crown.**

Then say: **While you are creating your jeweled crown, several members of your team may crumple the pieces of newspaper in your circle and may try to knock down the other teams' crowns. Team members may not step outside their crown circles. Remember, other groups will try to do the same to you. If your crown tumbles, your recorder will shout out the jewels you** have previously named as you restack your cans.

When one team has successfully built its kingly crown, has named a list of jewels, and has warded off any flying intrusions, the game is over. You may wish to set a time limit if the teams are not able to accomplish all three parts of the game.

Have the teams discuss the jewels that were placed in the crown of Jesus, the king. Read aloud 1 Timothy 6:15-16. Then ask:

- **What qualities should any king have?**
- **What makes Jesus a king?**
- **Why do we say, "Crown him with many crowns"?**
- **Which of Jesus' kingly qualities that your group named could you use more of this week? Why?**

Spread the Good News

SUMMARY: In this **learning game,** teenagers will experience the speed at which good news travels.

PREPARATION: You'll need a stopwatch or a watch with a second hand.

Have your entire group stand in a circle. The bigger the group, the better. Have teenagers take turns timing with the stopwatch, starting and stopping the watch on the words "go" and "stop."

Say: **Can you imagine how fast the news of the risen Christ spread on that first Easter morning? Let's see how quickly we can spread some good news. After I say "go," I'll turn to the person on my right, say "hallelujah!" and give** (name of person to your right) **a high five. Then** (name of person to your right) **will pass the signal—the high five and the "hallelujah"—to** (his or her) **neighbor. We'll continue this way around the circle. The last person in the circle will say "stop," and the timekeeper will let you know how long it took us to spread the good news.** After one round, say: **Let's try again to see if we can spread the news even faster.** The teenagers will want to keep trying to beat their old time.

You can vary this game by starting the hand signal going in both directions around the circle to see if it keeps going after it crosses. Or use signals such as squeezing hands, whistling, or elbow nudges around the circle. For another variation, try starting the round by squeezing hands in two directions with your eyes closed. Does the good news keep traveling?

When the kids have finished several rounds, say: **When Jesus' friends realized that he had risen from the tomb, they were excited! They just** *had* **to tell the others.** Ask:

- **Why does it appeal to us to help spread good or bad news quickly?**
- **How can spreading news turn into spreading hurtful gossip?**
- **What's one small way you can spread the good news of Jesus this week?**

Facts Are Facts

second time to coda

I know there's a God who knows— my name— and a Son who— died to take the blame. I— be-lieve Je-sus is com-in' back, 'cause prom-is-es are prom-is-es and facts are facts! Yeah! Prom-is-es are prom-is-es and facts are facts! Yeah, yeah!

That's right!

These— days, some— say there's no— one— way to be-lieve.—

Just keep— it loose; you're free to choose. There's no ab-so-lute; it's

all rel-a-tive, you see!— So I'm call-in' all de-fend-ers—

of the truth to live— a life that spells— out God's world view. Let

these words be heard— in ev-ery-thing— you say— and do!

Facts Are Facts

    Divide kids into two groups of equal size. Have one group form a circle and the other group form a line. During the verses, have the people in the line weave in and out between the people in the circle. Have the kids in the circle clap and stomp to the beat.

    For the chorus and the coda, have kids follow the parenthetical motions. The last time they repeat the chorus, have kids gradually sit down on the floor in relief.

Chorus:

(Find a partner from the opposite group, join hands, and walk in small circles during the first three lines of the chorus.)

I know there's a God who knows my name
And a Son who died to take the blame.
I believe Jesus is comin' back,
'Cause promises are promises and facts are facts! *(Shake hands with your partner in the traditional fashion on the first "promises," clasp thumbs and shake hands on the second "promises," give each other high fives on the first "facts," and "down low" fives for the second "facts.")*
Yeah! Promises are promises and facts are facts! *(Repeat handshakes and high fives.)*
Yeah, yeah! That's right! *(Return to your circle or line.)*

Coda:

As sure as there's a law of gravity *(lock wrists with your partner, and step in small circles)*
That says what goes up must come down *(keeping your wrists locked, stand toe to toe with your partner, lean back, and each sit down as far as you can go),*
This is the ultimate reality *(keeping your wrists locked, pull each other up):*
That God is *(bend knees),* and God loves *(stand straight),* and God can be found! *(Unlock wrists, and raise hands high.)*
Well, I know there's a God who knows my name! *(Clap to the beat.)*
Promises are promises and facts are facts! *(Shake hands with your partner in the traditional fashion on the first "promises," clasp thumbs and shake hands on the second "promises," give each other high fives on the first "facts," and "down low" fives for the second "facts.")*
And a Son who died to take the blame. *(Clap hands to the beat.)*
Promises are promises and facts are facts! *(Repeat handshakes and high fives.)*
And I believe Jesus, he's comin' back! *(Clap hands to the beat.)*

Flippin' Out!

SUMMARY: In this **learning game,** teenagers will discover the need for Bible-based decision making by flipping coins to run a relay.

PREPARATION: You'll need a Bible, two coins, and ten chairs. Arrange the chairs in two single-file rows from one end of the room to the other. Set the chairs approximately five feet apart next to each other and six feet apart across from each other (see diagram).

Gather kids at one end of the room, and divide the group in half. Line each team up single file behind a row of chairs. The first players in line should be standing about six feet behind the first chairs.

With both teams in place, hand each first player one coin. Say: **You are to run to the first chair and flip your coin. If it lands on "heads," run to the next chair. If it lands on "tails," you must run around the chair three times before moving on. Flip the coin at each chair. When you reach the other side of the room, touch the wall and then return to your team. Hand your coin to the next player, who will repeat the relay. The first team to finish wins!**

When the game is finished, ask:

● In what ways is flipping a coin like making a decision without knowing all the facts?

● What are some possible consequences of making decisions without first considering the results?

● What happens when a person has all the facts yet still chooses to make a poor decision? What happens to others close to him or her?

Have volunteers read aloud Joshua 1:8; Proverbs 3:5-6; and James 1:5. Ask:

● What can we do this week at home to make more God-led choices using Bible-based facts? at school? in our community?

Who Am I?

SUMMARY: In this **learning game**, teenagers will make masks to better understand how God knows them both inside and out.

PREPARATION: You'll need a Bible, scissors, whistle, pastel-colored construction paper, and markers. Cut the paper in the shape of a mask with two generic eyeholes. Do not cut out the mouth (see diagram). Make enough masks for all your kids.

Give each teenager a paper mask, and set out the markers on the floor for the kids to share. Explain that they'll use one side of their papers to make masks that reflect the ways they think others see them. Then they'll use the other side to make masks that reflect how they see themselves.

When everyone is finished, ask all of the kids to stand. Explain that they'll share their masks two ways.

First, while holding their masks in front of their faces, kids will portray the "outside" view and will use any voice other than their normal voice. They might sing, shout, cry, or talk like a robot, like a baby, or with a "country" accent.

For the second part, teenagers will flip their masks to display the "inside" view. They'll pantomime to portray this side. Each person will silently use appropriate body movements to communicate the meaning of his or her inner feelings.

Have kids start with the "outside" masks showing, and allow them ten seconds to share with as many people in as many ways as possible. Then blow the whistle. Have kids flip their masks and pantomime ten seconds more. Continue this for two minutes with ten-second intervals.

When time is up, have kids form a circle on the floor, and ask:

● What are some positive aspects of wearing masks? negative aspects?

● Are there times when appearance is more important than feelings?
Read aloud 1 Samuel 16:7. Then ask:

● How do you feel about God knowing us inside and out?

● How does wearing masks keep us from sharing the good news of Jesus?

Grin Again Gang

Grin a-gain, gang. Get gung-ho a-bout Je-sus.

Smile sweet-ly, Su-san, so you send Sa-tan sad-ly a-way.

Buck up, bro-ther Bill, be-cause a bunch of bit-ter boys be-come a bunch of bet-ter boys be-hind a

big, big smile. Grin a-gain, gang. Get gung-ho a-bout

1. Je-sus.

2. Je-sus.

Grin Again Gang

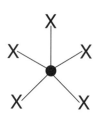

Have everyone get in a circle and face right. Have kids join left hands in the center of the circle and walk to the beat of the song. (See diagram at right.) Tell them to move faster and faster as they sing the song faster and faster.

VARIATIONS

● Each time kids repeat the song, have them face the opposite direction and place the opposite hands in the center of the circle.

● Have girls and guys form separate circles. Have everyone face right and then join left hands in the center of each circle. Tell both circles to move forward on "Grin again, gang. Get gung-ho about Jesus." Have girls only circle as they sing, "Smile sweetly, Susan, so you send Satan sadly away." Have guys only circle as they sing, "Buck up, brother Bill, because a bunch of bitter boys become a bunch of better boys behind a big, big smile." Have both circles move again as they sing, "Grin again, gang. Get gung-ho about Jesus."

● Have kids run an over-and-under relay while they sing this song. Kids pass items over their heads or in between their legs to the beat of the song. As the song gets faster and faster, kids pass the items faster and faster.

Have kids form two groups, and have each group form a line. Give the first person in each line a ball or a wad of paper. Have the first people pass the items over their heads to the people behind them. Then have those people pass the items between their legs to the people behind them, and so on, over and under, all the way to the end of the line. Have the last people take the items and run to the front of the lines and pass the items over their heads to continue the relay. Kids can relay to the beat of the song!

Connect-a-Smile!

SUMMARY: In this **just-for-fun game**, teenagers will try to make each other smile.

PREPARATION: None.

Select two people to be "It." Have everyone else spread out around the room. When everyone is in place, say: **The two who are It will try to make you smile to get you to join their team. They'll make silly faces, laugh, tell dumb jokes, or use whatever means necessary short of touching you in any way. Everything used to gain a smile must be in good taste, but most importantly, please avoid putting down other group members.**

Those who are not It will try to keep from smiling while they stand in place. If a person smiles, he or she must join It's team and place his or her hand on It's shoulder or the shoulder of the last person in line. New teammates may help make faces but must not let go. The game will continue until everyone has become part of a line. The winning team is the one with the longest line.

Play several rounds. You may want to award a prize to any person who manages to keep a straight face throughout the game.

The Tale of Happy and Sad

SUMMARY: In this **learning game,** teenagers will tell a story to show how attitude can draw others to Christ or can push them away.

PREPARATION: You'll need a Bible. You'll also need to arrange a circle of chairs, providing a chair for each person.

Have everyone sit in a chair; then say: **I'm going to start the story of "The Three Bears," and then I'll stop and point to one of you. The person I point to must continue the story in as positive a manner as possible. The person may laugh, jump up and down, or use whatever he or she wishes to tell that part of the story. After a few lines, the storyteller will stop and let the person to the left continue.**

That person will pick up where the previous storyteller left off to keep the story line intact. However, this person must tell the story in as negative a manner as possible. The story should remain the same, but this person may change expressions, stomp on the floor, scream, throw a fist in the air, or use anything else to convey a negative attitude. After a few lines, the storyteller will stop and let the person to the left continue on a positive note.

We'll continue this back-and-forth storytelling until we've circled the entire group twice to give each person the chance to play both positive and negative roles.

If you have a large group and the story ends before everyone has had a chance to play both roles, start a new story—"Red Riding Hood" or "The Three Little Pigs," for example. After everyone has shared twice, ask:

● **While telling the story, which role was easier to play—the positive or the negative? Why?**

● **Did the story seem to change when positive attitudes were used? If so, how?**

● **How did the story change with the negative attitudes?**

● **In what ways did you find yourself relating to those sharing positive parts of the story? negative parts?**

● **How might nonbelievers be drawn to or pushed away from positive Christians? negative Christians?**

Read aloud Philippians 2:5, 14-15 and 1 Timothy 4:12. Ask:

● **What can we do this week to present a positive attitude for those around us?**

Ain't Nobody

ARR. UBP.

Ain't Nobody

Have kids stand in a straight line and place their right hands on the right shoulders of the people in front of them. For the verses, have kids walk across the room in this position, following the parenthetical motions. When they reach the opposite side of the room, have them remain in the line, curve around, and walk the opposite direction.

For the chorus, have kids get out of the line and dance freestyle. At the end of the chorus, have kids take three large steps to get back into line.

1. I've got a friend, ain't nobody like him. *(Step right, left, right, left.)*
I've got a friend, ain't nobody like him. *(Step right, left, right, left.)*
I've got a friend, ain't nobody like him. *(Step right, left, right, left.)*
I've got a friend, ain't nobody like him. *(Step right, left, right, left.)*
Jesus, he's my friend *(lean forward, back, forward, back),*
Jesus, he's my friend. *(Lean forward, back, forward, back.)*

Words and music by Reggie Coates. Copyright 1985 Reggie Coates, P.O. Box 1764, Cupertino, CA 95015-1764. ARR. UBP.

More Than/Less Than

SUMMARY: In this **learning game**, kids will guess the answers to biblical trivia questions.

PREPARATION: For each team, label half a sheet of poster board "more than" on one side and "less than" on the other side. You'll need the list of biblical trivia questions on page 81 or your own list and a Bible. Have paper and a pen handy to keep score.

Divide the kids into at least three teams with no more than ten kids on a team, and have kids sit down with their teams.

Say: **We're going to play the More Than/Less Than game. I want one person from each team to stand up at the front of the room.** Give each person who's standing one of the poster board signs you made. **Say: I'm going to ask you a biblical trivia question, and you have to answer the question by holding up either the "more than" or "less than" side of your poster board. For example, I'll ask, "Was Joash more than or less than eight years old when he became king?"** (2 Kings 11:21). **Then you'll hold up the answer you believe to be correct. Everyone will get a turn to answer a question, and each person who answers correctly wins five points for his or her team. At the end of the game, the team with the most points wins.**

Play until each person has had a chance to stand up front to answer a question.

Encourage the teams to cheer on their teammates and even to shout out what they believe are the correct answers to help out their teammates.

After you've played a round, gather kids together, and ask:

● **How did the encouragement and support of your teammates help you with this game?**

● **How does Jesus support and encourage us with challenges we face in everyday life?**

● **How is your friendship with Jesus like earthly friendships? How is it different?**

Biblical Trivia Questions

1. **Was Joash more than/less than eight years old when he became king?** Answer: Less than (2 Kings 11:21—seven years old)

2. **Was the furnace more than/less than five times hotter than usual when Shadrach** (SHAYD-rak), **Meshach** (MEE-shack), **and Abednego** (a-BED-nee-go) **were thrown in?** Answer: More than (Daniel 3:19—seven times hotter)

3. **Did Joseph interpret more than/less than three dreams about the famine for Pharaoh?** Answer: Less than (Genesis 41:1-7, 25-32—two dreams)

4. **Did more than/less than four loaves of bread feed five thousand people?** Answer: More than (John 6:9—five loaves)

5. **Was Adam more than/less than 973 years old when he died?** Answer: Less than (Genesis 5:5—930 years old)

6. **Are there more than/less than sixty-three books of the Bible?** Answer: More than (sixty-six books)

7. **Did Moses send more than/less than eleven spies to explore the land of Canaan?** Answer: More than (Numbers 13:1-16—twelve spies)

8. **Was Noah more than/less than 300 years old when he began to build the ark?** Answer: More than (Genesis 5:32—more than 500 years old)

9. **When God vowed to divide Israel, did he say he would leave more than/less than twelve tribes to Solomon's son?** Answer: Less than (1 Kings 11:34-39—one tribe)

10. **Was Judas paid more than/less than forty pieces of silver to betray Jesus?** Answer: Less than (Matthew 27:3—thirty pieces of silver)

Shipping-Box Shuffle

SUMMARY: In this **just-for-fun game,** teams of teenagers will race with shipping boxes on their feet.

PREPARATION: You'll need two large shipping boxes for each relay team. Each box should be large enough to fit three teenage-sized feet in it. You can get boxes from a warehouse or can ask a manager at your local supermarket to save some for you. You'll also need masking tape to mark a starting point and an ending point on the floor for each team.

Have teenagers form groups of three; then have those groups form relay teams of up to nine people, depending on the size of your group. Have each relay team line up behind a piece of masking tape, and give each team two shipping boxes.

Say: **We're going to play the Shipping-Box Shuffle game. Three people on each team need to put their right feet together in one box and their left feet together in the other box. The object of the game is to "shuffle" or move the boxes forward to the ending point and then backward to the starting point. When you return to the starting point, get out of the boxes and let the next three people go. The first team whose members all complete the relay wins.**

If the teams do not have the same number of members, have some kids repeat the process so everyone can have a turn and so each team completes the same number of relays.

Sing Your Praise to the Lord

stand up and sing one more hal-le-lu-jah. Give your praise to the Lord! I can ne-ver tell you

just how much good that it's gon-na do ya just to sing, sing, sing. Come on

sing, sing, sing, let me hear ya now, sing, sing, sing.

Sing Your Praise to the Lord

Have kids form a front-to-back, single-file line on one end of the room, all facing the same direction.

For the chorus, have the kids lift their knees high as they step right, touch the left foot to the right foot, step left, then touch the right foot to the left foot. Next have kids walk across the room and then "peel off"—that is, every other person goes to either the right or the left.

For the verses, have kids stop where they are and do the parenthetical motions.

1. Just to sing anew *(raise right arm, then left arm)*
The song your heart learned to sing *(bring both arms down to sides)*
When he first gave his life to you. *(Raise right arm, then left arm.)*
The life goes on and so must the song. *(Bring both arms down to sides.)*
You gotta sing again *(raise right arm, then left arm)*
The song born in your soul *(bring both arms down to sides)*
When you first gave your heart to him. *(Raise right arm, then left arm.)*
Sing his praises once more. *(Bring both arms down to sides.)*

Adapted from J.S. Bach's Fugue No. 2 in C Minor. Words and music by Richard Mullins. © 1982 Meadowgreen Music Company/BMG Songs, Inc. (ASCAP). Meadowgreen Music Company admin. by EMI Christian Music Publishing. All rights reserved. Used by permission.

VARIATIONS

● Each time the kids say, "Sing, sing, sing," have them sing softly at first, then a little louder, then as loud as they can.

● Instead of lining up single file, have kids line up with a partner. Then have the partner on the right move to the right and the partner on the left move to the left.

● Between verses, have kids tell each other one-word ways that people praise the Lord—for example, "sing," "pray," "smile," or "love."

Puffed-Up Praise

SUMMARY: In this **learning game**, teenagers will see how praising God can fill them with joy.

PREPARATION: You'll need several stacks of newspapers, one large pair of sweat pants and a large sweat shirt for every three kids, an audiocassette or CD player, and a cassette tape or CD of praise music.

Have kids form groups of no more than three; then have each group choose a "puff person." Give each puff person a pair of oversized sweat pants and a sweat shirt, and instruct kids to put them on. Give each group a stack of newspapers.

Say: **While the music plays, we're going to praise God and "puff up" our puff people with joy. In your groups, take turns wadding up newspapers while you say things you appreciate about God. You might mention things such as "God, you're awesome" or "Thanks, God, for being so compassionate." Each time you mention a praise phrase, stuff a newspaper ball inside the sweats. We'll see which puff person can become the puffiest by the end of the song. Ready?**

Play an upbeat worship song such as "Sing Your Praise to the Lord" while kids play. When the song ends, have the puff people parade around the room before taking off the sweats and newspaper wads. Gather kids in a circle, and ask:

- **What was fun about praising God this way?**
- **What would have made the puff people even bigger?**

Say: **In this game, the puff people "grew" when you praised God.** Ask:

- **How do we grow when we praise God?**
- **Why does praising God fill us with joy?**

Say: **Turn to two people near you, and tell one way you'll praise God this week.** After kids have shared, close with a prayer similar to this one. Pray: **Dear God, thanks for being awesome and so worthy of our praises. Help us seek new ways to praise and worship you every day. Fill us with the joy that comes from worshiping you. Amen.**

Shootout at the Bad-Hair Corral

SUMMARY: In this **just-for-fun game**, teenagers will race to squirt hairstyling mousse off of balloon "bandits."

PREPARATION: You'll need a squirt gun with water for every two people, balloons, duct tape, and several containers of hairstyling mousse. This game is best played outside. Blow up at least one balloon for each person. Use duct tape to fasten the balloons to different items in your playing area, such as trees, fences, windowsills, or playground equipment.

Have kids form two groups, and send group 2 to the far end of the playing area. Have group 1 use the hairstyling mousse to create funky hairdos' on each balloon. While group 1 is "styling" the balloons, give each member of group 2 a squirt gun filled with water. When the balloons are ready, have members of group 1 gather in one area to watch the fun.

Say: **In this game, our playing area is an Old West town with lots of bad-hair bandits hiding in it. Members of group 2 are the hairstyle police who must "shave" each bad-hair bandit by squirting off the mousse hairdo. You'll have thirty seconds to shave as many bandits as you can. Then we'll see if group 1 can beat your record. Ready? Go!**

After thirty seconds, call time, and count the number of shaved bandits. Then have members of group 2 style the balloons while members of group 1 refill the squirt guns to play again.

Too Late

no   more   mid - dle   line._____   Oh,   it's
please   make   up   your   mind._____

too_____ late_____ for think - - ing   you can   walk the mid - dle   line,

bet- ter get wise._____

Too Late

Have kids form two straight lines, facing each other, about five feet apart.

For the chorus, have kids step right, bring feet together, step left, bring feet together, and so on, to the beat. At one end of the two lines, have the two end people walk or dance any way they want to down the middle of the lines and then join the lines at the other end. When they finish, have two more walk or dance down the middle.

For the verses, have kids follow the parenthetical motions.

1. **Oh, the time has come for making a decision** *(point to watch or clock),*
And you say you found the light. *(Hold both hands up, and look up.)*
But the talk is cheap when I see the way you're living *(shake right index finger),*
Walking in the night. *(Close eyes, and place hands out as if walking blindly.)*

2. **You may think you can live by your feelings** *(tap right index finger on forehead),*
Different every night. *(Place both arms out to sides.)*
But an emotional religion will crumble at our feet *(crouch down)*
If we're made to stand and fight. *(Stand up, and get in any kind of "fighting position.")*

VARIATIONS

● Instead of doing actions for the verses, kids can dance freestyle and clap hands to the beat.

● Between verses, have kids switch places with the person facing them in the opposite line. Have them give each other high fives as they pass each other in the center.

● Instead of walking down the middle of two lines, place a strip of masking tape down the center of your room. During the chorus, have kids walk along the masking tape line.

Balloon Bash

SUMMARY: In this **just-for-fun game**, blindfolded team members will race to stomp balloons in the proper order at the direction of team members who can see.

PREPARATION: You'll need blindfolds, a large bag of balloons, and a marker. Before the game, blow up ten balloons for every team, and mark them with the numbers one through ten.

Divide your group into teams of at least two and not more than ten. Separate each team into a different corner of the room.

Say: **The object of this game is simple. I'll give each team ten numbered balloons, and the first team that stomps their balloons in correct numerical order will win. The catch is that only half the team can do the stomping, and that half will be wearing blindfolds. The other half of the team will direct them to the correct balloons using only the words "left," "right," "forward," "stop," and "stomp."**

To begin, make sure half of each team is blindfolded. Circle each blindfolded person around several times, scatter the balloons near their feet, and say "go!"

Whose Side Are You On?

SUMMARY: In this **learning game**, teenagers must discover who their teammates are to learn a lesson about making a decision for Christ.

PREPARATION: You'll need three or four decks of cards, a few tables, slips of paper, and a pencil. Each member of the group will need a slip of paper. On half of the slips, write this instruction: "You may not speak. Join with at least three other people, and begin work on a house of cards. When the house is four levels tall, your team will win the game." On the remaining slips, write this instruction: "You may not speak. Join with at least three other people, and begin work on a house of cards. Your house may be only two levels tall. Do not let anyone build higher. When you use all your cards, your team wins."

Set half a deck of cards on each table. Mix up the instructions, and give a slip of paper to each person. Say: **Read and follow what's written on your slip of paper, and don't share it with anyone else. The first team to complete its assignment wins the game. Feel free to move around the room as often as you need to.**

After the game, ask:

● **How did you feel when you discovered that other people were play-ing by different rules?**

● **How did you find the right team?**

● **Some people say it's impossible to keep one foot in the world and one foot in the kingdom of God. Do you agree or disagree?**

Spot the Spitballer

SUMMARY: In this **just-for-fun game**, teenagers will identify guilty spitballers.

PREPARATION: You'll need drinking straws for everyone and sever-al sheets of paper.

Have the group sit facing the same direction, as in a classroom. Ask for a volunteer to be the "substitute teacher." Say: **When our substitute's back is turned, take turns shooting wads of paper at her** (or his) **back—no real spit, please! When the teacher turns around, she'll** (he'll) **try to guess who shot the spitball by examining your facial expressions.** If the guess is correct, the substitute and student trade places. If the substitute is wrong, he or she turns around and waits for the next spitball.

JOY!

Joy!

Have teenagers form two groups.

For the verses, when each group sings "joy," "love," or "light," have that group's members raise their arms in the air and then lower them; the two groups should be alternately raising and lowering their arms while singing their parts. For the verses, the words for group 2 appear in parentheses.

For the chorus, have kids follow the parenthetical motions.

1. I got the joy (joy), joy (joy), joy (joy).
I got the joy (joy), joy (joy), joy (joy).
I got the joy (joy), joy (joy), joy.

Chorus:

ALL: **Two! Three! Four!** *(Motion with fingers "two," "three," and "four.")*
GROUP 1: **Down in my heart** *(make fists, bend arms, and bring arms down twice facing slightly to the right; then clap twice),*
GROUP 2: **Down in my heart** *(make fists, bend arms, and bring arms down twice facing slightly to the left; then clap twice),*
GROUP 1: **Down in my heart to stay** *(make fists, bend arms, and bring arms down twice facing slightly to the right; then give a "thumbs up" on the word "stay"),*
GROUP 2: **Down in my heart to stay.** *(Make fists, bend arms, and bring arms down twice facing slightly to the left; then give a "thumbs up" on the word "stay.")*

2. I got the love (love), love (love), love (love).
I got the love (love), love (love), love (love).
I got the love (love), love (love), love.

3. I got the light (light), light (light), light (light).
I got the light (light), light (light), light (light).
I got the light (light), light (light), light.

4. I got the joy (joy), joy (joy), joy (joy).
I got the joy (joy), joy (joy), joy (joy).
I got the joy (joy), joy (joy), joy.

Words by George W. Cook. Music by Amy Grant. © 1993 Age To Age Music, Inc., ASCAP (admin. by BH Publishing), et al. All Rights Reserved. Used By Permission.

VARIATIONS

● Have kids sing new verses according to the topics you're studying, such as "grace" or "peace."

● After the first "joy" verse, have each person quickly find a partner and do anything—no touching allowed—to make his or her partner laugh. Kids can make the craziest face or do the most bizarre motion; then they should switch to give each partner a turn.

● During the "light" verse, have a volunteer flick the room lights on and off.

● Have kids form three groups, and assign each group the number "two," "three" or "four." Each time they sing their number, they should jump in the air.

Give It Away

SUMMARY: In this **learning game**, teenagers will play the game Competition Hot Potato to learn a lesson about sharing joy.

PREPARATION: You'll need a sack of potatoes (about a dozen). You may substitute balls or beanbags.

Have kids form teams of at least four but not more than six. Give each team two or three potatoes, and have each team form a circle. Say: **Today we're going to play Competition Hot Potato. The object of the game is to keep the potatoes moving. If you hold onto a potato for more than a second, your team is out. If you drop a potato, your team is out. The team that keeps its potatoes flying the longest wins.**

Award the potatoes to the winning team. Then ask:
● How is playing Hot Potato like spreading joy?
● What was it like to drop a potato or hold onto it too long?
● How is that like not keeping joy alive in your life?
● What can we do to keep joy alive in our group?
● What are some things we do that keep joy from spreading?
● How can we spread joy outside our group?

Secret Joy

SUMMARY: In this **learning game**, teenagers will discover what gives other people joy.

PREPARATION: You'll need an Almond Joy candy bar for a prize.

Gather the group together. Say: **Today we're going to learn a little bit more about the things that give us joy. I'd like each of you to think of one thing that gives you joy. For example, it might be Mom, Dad, friends, pizza, or your pet. You can make it easy or difficult. Don't tell anyone what you're thinking.**

Wait a moment, and then say: **Now I want you to find out what gives other people joy. Take turns asking each other "yes-or-no" questions. When you find out what gives someone joy, he or she must shout "hallelujah!" The first person to find out what gives five people joy wins.**

Give the winner an Almond Joy candy bar. Then ask:
● We're all different, but we have some things in common. What are some of the things that give almost everyone joy?
● What are some ways we can have more joy?
● Is there a difference between joy and fun? If so, what?
● What are some ways we can share our joy with others?

Great and Mighty Is He

Great and Mighty Is He

For the chorus, have kids bend their knees to the beat and clap to the beat. For the verses, have kids follow the parenthetical motions.

1. **Let us lift his name up high** *(raise both arms above head),*
Celebrate his grace *(keep both arms up and wave hands);*
For he has redeemed our lives *(bring both arms down to sides),*
And he reigns *(raise both arms to waist level)* **on high.** *(Raise both arms above head.)*

VARIATIONS

● Have kids play guitars and other instruments the first time they sing the chorus and verse. The second time they sing the chorus and verse, have them clap hands instead of play the instruments. Then to close the song, have them play instruments again.

● Instruct teenagers to begin the song by singing softly and then to gradually sing louder.

● During verse 1, let the kids use anything wooden—wooden spoons, wooden blocks, broom handles, pencils, or table tops, for example—for percussion. During verse 2, let kids use anything metal, such as coins against a cabinet, spoons, pans, or folding chairs.

● Give each person a sheet of paper. Have kids snap the paper out for percussion.

Lead From Behind

SUMMARY: In this **just-for-fun game**, one teenager will lead his or her blindfolded teammates through a maze, giving directions from the back of the line.

PREPARATION: You'll need a roll of wide masking tape, blindfolds (up to nine, depending on the size of your group), a stopwatch, and a bag of candy. Before the game, use the masking tape to create a simple maze on the floor that measures about fifteen feet square. The path should be about two feet wide.

Have kids form teams of at least two but not more than ten. Explain that each team will navigate the maze in turn.

Invite the first team to line up at the beginning of the maze. Have each team member put on a blindfold except for the last person in line. When team members are blindfolded, ask them to put their hands on the shoulders of the people directly in front of them. Say: **When I say "go," the last person in line will direct you through the maze. If anyone in the team crosses a masking tape boundary, the whole team must back up and start again. The team with the best time wins.**

Keep time with the stopwatch, and award a bag of candy to the winners.

What's It Worth?

SUMMARY: In this **learning game**, teenagers will learn about the value of common objects and will discuss why we place a high value on praising God.

PREPARATION: You'll need index cards, several markers, and a table. Purchase five objects that you can use both in the game and as prizes to the winners, such as a bag of M&M's, a can of fruit, a bag of balloons, a six-pack of soda, or a bag of chips.

Write the price of each object on an index card, and line up the merchandise on a table. Place each index card face down on the table under the appropriate item.

Have kids form teams of at least two but not more than ten. Give each team a small stack of index cards and a marker. Say: **Today we're going to play a game similar to** *The Price Is Right.* **As a team, you have to guess the price of each object and write it down. The team with the best guess—without going over—wins that item.**

After the game, ask these questions:
- **Why is it important to know what things are worth?**
- **How do we find out how much something is worth?**
- **How much is your relationship with God worth?**
- **What does praising God have to do with how much we value him?**

Aerospace Race

SUMMARY: In this **just-for-fun game**, teams will compete to send a balloon the greatest distance.

PREPARATION: You'll need a balloon and the following items for each team: a plastic spoon, one foot of masking tape, ten feet of twine, a thick rubber band, a paper clip, and a drinking straw.

Have kids form teams of at least two but not more than ten. Give each team a balloon and the other six items listed above. Say: **Let's see which team can send a balloon the greatest distance. You may use any of the materials I've given you in any way you like—as long as it's safe.**

Give the teams ten minutes to create a plan; then let them demonstrate their projects one at a time. Give the winners the remaining balloons.

Never Giving Up

preach-er said___ on   Sun-day   that   we should   watch   and

pray,___   and   don't you   let the   de-vil   stop you on___ the

way.   Don't get   tired of   wait-ing;   the

Word of   God   is   true.___   Just the way___ he

said he   would, he'll   come for   me   and   you.___

D.S. al Coda

102

Never Giving Up

Since this song has a "country" feel to it, try a few square-dancing steps with the kids. For verse 1, have kids join hands and circle to the right. For verse 2, have kids join hands and circle to the left. For verse 3, have kids join hands and circle to the right.

For the chorus, have kids face partners, hook right arms and circle to the right. Each time you sing the chorus, have kids find a different partner, hook right arms, and circle to the right.

VARIATIONS

● Have partners alternate singing, "Never, never, never," or have guys and girls alternate singing.

● Instead of hooking elbows with a partner, kids could find a partner and do-si-do. To do-si-do, face your partner and walk around each other, passing right shoulders and then back to back. Then move to your original place, passing left shoulders.

● During the music between verses, have kids quickly tell a partner one reason they're not giving up on God.

Lockup!

SUMMARY: In this **just-for-fun game**, teenagers will lock arms with one another by running back and forth across a room.

PREPARATION: If your room is not square, you'll need to make it so by laying a ten-foot masking tape line.

	TEAM 1	TEAM 2	
	X	X	
	X	X	
	X	X	
TEAM 3 X X X			X X X TEAM 3
TEAM 4 X X X			X X X TEAM 4
	X	X	
	X	X	
	X	X	
	TEAM 1	TEAM 2	

Divide your group into four equal teams, and number the groups 1 through 4. If a team has an uneven number of players, one player will have to run twice. Split each team in half, and place them at opposite ends of the room, using all four sides of the room or masking tape square. Ask teams members to line up in single file.

When everyone is in place, explain how Lockup! works. Say: **The first person on one half of the team will run and lock arms with the first teammate in line on the opposite side of the room. Both of you will then return to the starting side and lock arms with the next player on your team. This back-and-forth running will continue until your whole team is connected.**

All four teams will be running at the same time. You may not touch a player on another team at any time during play.

Explain that once all team members have been connected, the group is to sit on the floor and yell "lockup!" to win.

Trust Train

SUMMARY: In this **learning game**, blindfolded teenagers will form a train to discover the importance of perseverance through temptation.

PREPARATION: You'll need a Bible and one blindfold for each person.

Have kids spread out around the room, and give each person a blindfold.

Choose one person to be the "engine," and have the rest of the kids put on their blindfolds.

Say: **Starting with the "engine," your group will make a human train. The goal is to make the train go as fast as possible. The engine will stand silently while the rest of you move slowly, saying, "Choo-choo?" Try to find the engine to become part of the human train. The identifying signal is silence. When you bump into someone, you both must exchange "Choo-choos?" If both players respond, you must move on.**

Whoever bumps into the engine first starts the train by taking hold of the engine's waist or the waist of the last person in line. After joining the engine, the players will become silent like the engine. As each person joins the line, the engine leads them to another part of the room to stand silently until the next person finds them and joins the line. **Keep your blindfolds on during the game.**

Start the game, and continue until everyone has joined the train. Have kids remove their blindfolds. then ask:

● **Was there anything frustrating about this activity? If so, what and why?**

● **Were you ever tempted to remove your blindfold? If so, how did it feel to want to give in to that temptation?**

● **If you weren't tempted, how did it feel to succeed in playing by the rules?**

Read aloud James 1:2-8 and Colossians 3:1-3. Ask:

● **What does this say about following God, whom we can't see?**

● **What happens the longer we endure and resist temptation?**

● **How can we resist personal temptation this week?**

Balloon Bop

SUMMARY: In this **just-for-fun game**, teenagers will try to keep "stone-filled" balloons aloft.

PREPARATION: You'll need three marbles and three uninflated balloons. Place a marble in each balloon, inflate the balloons, and tie them off.

Have kids divide into three teams, and have each team stand in a circle and hold hands.

Toss a marble-filled balloon into the air for each group as you say: **Keep the balloon in the air without letting go of each other's hands.** The marble-filled balloon will move in unexpected ways. Congratulate the team that's able to keep the balloon in the air the longest.

I Am a "C"

I Am a "C"

Have everyone begin the song by sitting in a chair. Each time the kids sing a letter, have one person stand up. If everyone in your group is standing before you reach the end of the song, have kids sit down, one at a time, each time the group sings a letter. At the end of the song, have everyone jump and shout, "I am a C!"

VARIATIONS

● Each time kids sing the song, instruct them to sing it faster and faster and then slower and slower. Instead of having kids stand and sit to the beat, have them stomp or clap.

● Have kids "follow the leader" to do actions. Choose someone to start the song, and ask that person to think of an action for each line that all the others have to follow—for example, stand up and wave both hands or jump in a 180-degree circle.

● Between repetitions, have kids pantomime actions that show they're Christians, such as praising God, giving hugs, or kneeling in prayer.

● Have teenagers sing the song as they'd sing "Bingo," clapping in place of singing a letter. Have them continue until they eventually clap the entire spelling of "Christian"—for example, "I am a (clap). I am a (clap)-H. I am a (clap)-H-R-I-S-T-I-A-N."

Bible-Character Scramble

SUMMARY: In this **just-for-fun game**, teenagers will form a famous Bible duo by finding their matches and locating their stories in the Bible.

PREPARATION: You'll need Bibles and a list of characters from the Bible. Each character should be part of a pair, such as Samson and Delilah, Ruth and Boaz, Abraham and Sarah, Adam and Eve, Noah and Mrs. Noah, and so on. Write each name on a slip of paper, and mix up the slips in a bowl or hat.

Have each person draw a name out of the hat, but tell kids not to show their names to anyone else. Say: **Your biblical character is part of a pair. You must find the person who has your character's match by shouting out the name of who you think is your character's other half. When you have found your partner, quickly try to find a passage in the Bible where your names appear together. The first couple to find each other and the passage wins!**

Ice-Cream Soccer

SUMMARY: In this **just-for-fun game**, teenagers will play a game of coffee-can soccer while making ice cream.

PREPARATION: You'll need a recipe for homemade ice cream (see recipe on page 109); two clean, empty coffee cans with lids (one large and one small); a bag of crushed ice; a bag of rock salt; and a roll of duct tape. The following recipe will feed ten to twelve kids. If you have a larger group, you'll need extra supplies. You'll need to play this game outside, so mark off goals to create a soccer field. Have bowls and spoons ready so everyone can enjoy the ice cream after the game!

Have kids mix the ingredients to make the ice cream and pour the mixture into the small coffee can. Tape the small can securely shut, and place it inside the larger coffee can. Surround the small can with ice and salt, and then tape the large can securely shut. The kids can now play soccer with the can. Rolling and agitating the can causes the milk mixture to turn into ice cream—and kids can play "soccer" while they wait! The process takes about forty-five minutes, and you should stop the game about every ten minutes to put in more ice and salt. Have fun, and enjoy the fruits of your labor!

HOMEMADE ICE CREAM
4 eggs
2½ cups of sugar
6 cups of milk
4 cups of light whipping cream
2 tablespoons of vanilla
½ teaspoon salt

Beat the eggs; then add sugar gradually until the mixture thickens. Add the remaining ingredients, and mix thoroughly. Pour into coffee cans. Makes 1 gallon.

Frisbee Soccer

SUMMARY: In this **learning game**, teenagers will play a variation of soccer without knowing who their team members are.

PREPARATION: You'll need a Frisbee, two trash cans set up as goals, and a slip of paper for each person with either "team A" or "team B" written on it.

Give each person a slip of paper to let them know what team they're on, but tell kids to keep their team identity a secret. At the playing area, tell kids which goal is for team A and which is for team B. Explain that each team should try to score by tossing the Frisbee to team members and into the goal; remind kids not to say what team they're on. Tell kids that they may move around and play defense but they cannot touch others. Throw the Frisbee into the group to begin.

After the game, ask:

● **What made this game difficult?**

● **Describe situations in which our identity is crucial to our success.**

● **How is our identity with Christ crucial to our success in our Christian lives?**

Pharaoh, Pharaoh

Words and music by Tony Sbrana. Copyright © 1971 Songs & Creations, Inc., P.O. Box 7, San Anselmo, CA 94979. All world rights reserved. UBP. Used by permission.

C   **F**   **G**

bur - ning bush told me just the oth - er day that
'n' God's peo - ple com - in' to the Red Sea, and
Phar - aoh's ar - my is a - com - in', too, so

C   **F**   **G** **F** **C**   **F**

I should come ov - er here and stay. Got - ta get my peo - ple out - ta
Phar - aoh's ar - my com - in' a - fter me. I raised my rod and stuck it
what do you think that I did do? I raised my rod, and I

G **F** **C**   **F**   **G** **F**   *D.C. al Coda*

Phar - aoh's hand and lead them all to the Prom - ised Land. I said...
in the sand; all of God's peo - ple walked a - cross dry land. I said...
cleared my throat, and all of Phar - aoh's ar - my did the dead - man's float. I said...

CODA **G**   3   **F**   3   **C**

Yeah, yeah, yeah, yeah. Yeah!

111

Pharaoh, Pharaoh

For the chorus and the verses, have kids follow the parenthetical motions.

Chorus:

Pharaoh, Pharaoh (make "Egyptian motions" to the right and then to the left),

Ooh (form a big "O" with both arms over your head), **baby** (bring the same O down low and rock it like you're cradling a baby),

Let my people go! (Use both thumbs to point to yourself; then point both index fingers out on "go.")

Uh! (Make fists, bend arms, and bring arms down to sides.)

Yeah, yeah, yeah, yeah. (Make "rain movement" with fingers, starting overhead and coming down.)

1. **Well a burning bush told me just the other day** (cup hands by ears)
That I should come over here and stay. (Motion, "Come here"; then point straight down.)
Gotta get my people outta Pharaoh's hand (hold both hands out)
And lead them all to the Promised Land. (Motion, "Forward ho" with right arm.)
I said...

2. **Well me 'n' God's people comin' to the Red Sea** (point to self, then point over shoulder, then make swimming motions),
And Pharaoh's army comin' after me. (Look over your right shoulder.)
I raised my rod (raise right hand as if holding a rod) **and stuck it in the sand** (make a downward stabbing motion with "rod");
All of God's people walked across dry land. (Walk in place.)
I said...

3. **Well Pharaoh's army is a-comin', too** (place one hand over heart, as if panicking),
So what do you think that I did do? (Hold hands up and out to side and shrug shoulders.)
I raised my rod and cleared my throat (raise rod with one hand, and hold throat with the other hand),
And all of Pharaoh's army did the dead-man's float. (Place both arms overhead and lean forward as if doing a front float.)
I said...

Yeah! (Raise both hands overhead, and make rain motion.)

Mortar Mess

SUMMARY: In this gooey **learning game**, each group of "Israelites" will make its own "clay brick and mortar."

PREPARATION: You'll need Bibles, two large bowls, four cups of dirt, four cups of water, measuring cups, two loaf pans, an open space outside, and water and towels for wiping hands. Place the bread pans about twenty feet away from the gathering area, and keep all the other supplies at your meeting place.

Have kids open their Bibles and read together Exodus 1:6-14. Then have them form two groups, and have each group gather around a bowl.

Say: **When the Israelites were slaves in Egypt, they were forced to make bricks and mortar to help build Egyptian cities. Now you'll get your chance to be just like the Israelite slaves! Remember, slaves must work quickly. The Egyptians are watching. Each group will measure out two cups of dirt and two cups of water into its bowl, adding more dirt or water to make its "mortar" the consistency of cement. The best mortar has to be mixed by hand. After the mortar is thoroughly mixed, each member of the group will take a turn carrying one handful of the mortar to the bread pan until all the mortar is in the bread pan. Only one slave at a time may be carrying mortar from each group. When all of the mortar is in the pan and formed into a brick, turn the pan over, pop out the brick, and you're finished!**

While teenagers are washing up, ask:

● **What job in your life do you consider despicable?**

● **Just as there was in the Israelite's time, there is injustice among people today. Why?**

● **How can you make even a small, positive difference against society's injustice today?**

People Piles

SUMMARY: In this **just-for-fun game,** teenagers will get to know each other better by answering "yes-or-no" questions.

PREPARATION: You'll need a chair for each teenager.

Have teenagers sit in chairs that have been arranged in a large circle. Begin by asking a question aloud that can be answered "yes" or "no," and tell teenagers to silently answer the question. Tell them that if they answered "no," they should stay seated. But if they answered "yes," they should move one seat to the right. If the chair on the right is already occupied, they'll need to sit on a lap. Continue around the circle, allowing each person to ask appropriate yes-or-no questions. You may develop "people piles" quite quickly. The game ends when everyone returns to a single chair or when you can't think of any more yes-or-no questions.

Here are some sample questions to get you started:

● **Have you ever kissed your dog or your cat on the lips?**

● **Have you ever stood in front of a mirror and sung with a pretend microphone?**

● **Have you ever tasted frog legs?**

● **Is science your favorite subject?**

● **Do you talk on the telephone more than an hour a day?**

Love Carrier

It's all right. It's all right. Wo, wo, wo,

wo, wo, it's all right. It's all right.

Car-ri-er, car-ri-er, if you need a car-ri-er, it's all right. It's all right.

Car-ri-er, car-ri-er, Je-sus is the car-ri-er.___ It's all right.___

Words and music by Billy Crockett and Kenny Wood. Copyright © 1989 by Word Music (a div. of Word, Inc.). All rights reserved. International copyright secured. Used by permission.

Gm7   Am7   B♭ C F   *Fine*

Liv-ing love, giv-ing love, love car-ri- er._____

Got a fist full of
He's got a heart full of

F   F

fear,   and you can't let it go.
love,   and you can't stop the flow.

And your heart says
He's got a dream for the

Am   Dm   Gm   C

jump,   but you just don't know._____
world   that he wants you to know._____

So you still play the
Take a chance on the

F   C   Am   Dm   B♭

game,   but you're tired of the show.   Oh,____   you
love   when your heart says go.   Oh,____   it's

F   C   F   *1st time D.S.* C7
                                                           2nd time D.S. al FINE

got- ta make a move;   don't you need a car-ri- er?_____
time to make a move;   we all need a car-ri- er._____

Love Carrier

For the introduction and chorus, have kids follow the parenthetical motions.

For the verses, designate a leader, and have kids joins hands. Have the leader spiral the line to the center of the room and then unspiral it back to the original position.

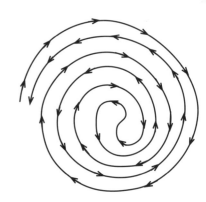

It's all right. *(Guys sing and raise both arms and punch the air twice.)*
It's all right. *(Girls sing and raise both arms and punch the air twice.)*
Wo, wo, wo, wo, wo *(all sing and turn in individual circles),*
It's all right. *(Guys sing and raise both arms and punch the air twice.)*
It's all right. *(Girls sing and raise both arms and punch the air twice.)*

Chorus:

Carrier, carrier, if you need a carrier *(all sing and clap to the beat),*
It's all right. *(Guys sing and raise both arms and punch the air twice.)*
It's all right. *(Girls sing and raise both arms and punch the air twice.)*
Carrier, carrier, if you need a carrier *(all sing and clap to the beat),*
It's all right. *(Guys sing and raise both arms and punch the air twice.)*
It's all right. *(Girls sing and raise both arms and punch the air twice.)*
Carrier, carrier, Jesus is the carrier. *(All sing and clap to the beat.)*
It's all right. *(Continue clapping.)*
Living love *(guys sing and raise both arms and punch the air twice),*
Giving love *(girls sing and raise both arms and punch the air twice),*
Love carrier. *(All sing and clap.)*

VARIATIONS

● On the last spiral, have everyone squeeze in for a group hug.

● Instead of spiraling, have kids join hands and follow each other into a different room during each verse.

The Love Train

SUMMARY: In this **learning game,** teenagers will try to put 1 Corinthians 13:4-8 in the correct order.

PREPARATION: You'll need to write out each verse of 1 Corinthians 13:4-8 on a separate index card. For example, write "Love is patient and kind. Love is not jealous, it does not brag, and it is not proud." on one card. Write out the whole passage, one verse at a time per card, ending with "Love never ends." for verse 8. Don't include any Scripture references. Then start over again until there is one card per teenager. Fold each card in half.

Distribute one folded index card to each person. Ask kids not to read the cards until the game begins. Say: **Each card has a portion of 1 Corinthians 13:4-8 written on it. When I say "go," read your card and then complete the passage by finding four other people who have the other verses of the** passage written on their cards. When you have five people who have different verses of the passage, the five of you must line up from left to right in the correct order and yell, "Love train!" Ready? Go!

When the first group yells, "Love train!" have that group read its cards. If they are in correct order, have them wait for the rest of the groups to finish. If they are not in the correct order, have them try again. Continue until almost everyone has put the verse together correctly.

After the game, ask:

● **What was your reaction to this activity?**

● **How is working with others to put these verses together like carrying love to each other in real life?**

● **In what ways did Jesus exemplify these verses while he was here on earth?**

● **How can we show and share Christ's love with others?**

Piggyback Race

SUMMARY: In this **learning game,** teenagers will carry teammates who are holding cups of water.

PREPARATION: You'll need a small paper cup for each person, three empty two-liter plastic bottles, water, three chairs, and three small tables. Set the chairs at one end of the room about ten feet apart, and put the tables at the opposite end of the room. Place the plastic bottles on the table.

Have kids form three teams. Have each team line up from the shortest person to the tallest next to a table with a plastic bottle on it. Give each person a cup filled with water. Have the first person in each line set aside his or her cup for a later time.

Say: **When I say "go," carry your teammate piggyback across to the chair. Circle the chair three times. Then put your teammate down, and take his or her cup of water. Balance the cup of water on your head while you and your teammate race back to the line together. When you get to the line, pour the water into the plastic bottle. Then the person who was carried has to carry the next person and repeat the process.** Be sure that the first person who carried a teammate returns to the end of the line with a cup of water to have his or her turn at being carried. At the end of the relay, the team that filled its plastic bottle with the most water wins.

After the game ask:

● **Was it more difficult to carry someone or to be carried? Explain.**

● **Which was easier: being carried and trying not to spill any water or letting your teammate balance the water for you?**

Say: **Jesus is like the teammate who carried you, and the water is like the burdens of the world you carry around.**

● **What are some things you are dealing with that are weighing you down?**

Say: **Jesus not only wants to carry you through difficult times, he wants to carry your burdens for you, too. But you have to give them to him first. Let's pray and ask Jesus to help us let go of one worry so he can carry it for us.**

I'm Not Ashamed

Lyrics:

I'm not a-shamed to let you know. I want this light in me to show. I'm not a-shamed to speak the name of Je-sus Christ.

1. What are we sneak-ing a-round for? Who are we try-ing to please?

Shrug-ging off sin, a - po - lo - giz - ing like we're

spread-ing some kind of di-sease. I'm say - ing, "No way,

no way." I'm not a-shamed

This one says it's a lost cause; save your tes-ti-mon - ies for church-

time. The o-ther ones state, "You'd bet-ter wait un-til you

119

do a lit-tle mar-ket re-search." I'm say - ing, "No way,

no way." I'm not a-shamed

to let you know. I want this light in me to show.

I'm not a-shamed to speak the name of Je-sus Christ.

I'm not a-shamed to speak the name of Je-sus Christ.

I'm Not Ashamed

For the chorus, have kids stand in a circle, face the center, join hands, and perform the parenthetical motions.

For the verses, have kids stay in the circle, face the center, and place their arms around each other's shoulders. Then have kids do the grapevine: Step right, left foot behind, right, left foot in front, right, left foot behind, right, left foot in front, and so on, continuing throughout each verse.

Chorus:

I'm not ashamed to let you know. *(Keeping hands joined, walk halfway toward the center of the circle.)*
I want this light in me to show. *(In the center of the circle, lift clasped hands high.)*
I'm not ashamed to speak the name of Jesus Christ. *(Keeping hands joined, lower arms as you walk backward to original place.)*

VARIATIONS

● Have kids shake their heads and shout, "No way, no way!" at the appropriate time during the song.

● Have kids brainstorm about ways people use their heads or hands to say, "No way." For example, kids can shake their heads from side to side or shake their heads and motion with their arms when they sing, "no way" during the song.

● Instead of doing the song in a large circle, have kids form three small circles to do the song.

● Have kids stand in place and clap during the verses. Assign a volunteer to stand in the center of the circle and pantomime the words. Then at the end of the verse, have the kids forming the circle point their fingers at the volunteer and shout, "No way, no way!"

Bumper Cars

SUMMARY: In this **just-for-fun game,** teenagers will try to bump other pairs out of the playing area.

PREPARATION: You'll need masking tape, inner tubes, and skateboards.

Before this activity, use masking tape to mark off a ten-by-twenty-foot playing area. You may need a larger playing area if you have more than ten players.

Have kids form pairs, and give each pair an inner tube and a skateboard. If you're short on supplies, have kids form trios. In each pair, have one partner sit or squat on the skateboard so his or her feet don't touch the ground. Then say: **If you're riding on a skateboard, slip the inner tube over your head and around your middle to create a bumper car. Your partner** (or partners) **will push on your shoulders to guide you in this game. If your car hits someone who is pushing, your car is out.**

Explain that partners will have one minute to bump other bumper cars out of the playing area. When a car is bumped out, it must stay there until the next round. After one minute, have partners switch roles and play again.

If your bumper cars are falling over rather than being bumped out of the playing area, have the partners push from the side and aim for the front or back of other skateboards rather than for the sides.

Pay the Price

SUMMARY: In this **learning game**, teenagers will perform awkward tasks to free "hostages."

PREPARATION: You'll need slips of paper, a pencil, two cups, and a watch with a second hand. Write five or six silly instructions on separate slips of paper. You might include tasks such as "Sing 'You Are My Sunshine,' " "Have each person in your group say his or her name backward," or "Act like a ballerina." You'll need a set of five or six actions for two groups. (The sets can be identical.)

Have teenagers form two groups, and say: **Each group may take "hostage" two members of the other group. Send your hostages to one corner of the room.** Wait for kids to follow your instructions; then continue: **To free your team members, everyone in your group must follow the instructions on these slips of paper faster than the other group. I'll time both groups to see who completes the assignment the fastest.**

Give each group a cup with the instruction slips in it. Have groups take turns acting out all the instructions while you time them. Everyone in the group must participate in each instruction. Then free all the hostages. Ask:

● **How did you feel while you acted out the instructions?**
● **Why did you act them out?**

Say: **Some of you might have been embarrassed to follow the instructions. That's the same way some people feel about talking about Jesus.** Have a volunteer read 2 Timothy 1:8-9. Ask:

● **What does this passage say about sharing your faith with others?**
● **Why are some people embarrassed to talk about Jesus?**
● **When is it hard for you to talk about Jesus? What would make it easier?**
● **What motivates you to share your faith?**

Say: **Great things happen when we're not ashamed to tell others how Jesus freed us from sin.**

Shut De Do

good and bad   was just   a game.   (Shut de do,   keep de   de-vil in de night.)
hun-gry for   a soul   to hurt.   (Shut de do,   keep de   de-vil in de night.)
Pa-pa used   to sing   it too.   (Shut de do,   keep de   de-vil in de night.)

Ma-ny years   and ma-ny tri-als,   (Shut de do,   keep   out de de-vil.) they
And with-out   your ho-ly ar-mor,   (Shut de do,   keep   out de de-vil.)
Je-sus called   and took   them home,   (Shut de do,   keep   out de de-vil.) and

3rd time to Coda

proved to me   they're not   the same.   (Shut de do,   keep de   de-vil in de night.)
he will   eat you   for dessert.   (Shut de do,   keep de   de-vil in de night.)
so I sing   this song   for you.   (Shut de do,   keep de   de-vil in de night.)

G   C   D   G   C   D

Bridge

Hey,   hey,   hey!   Shut de do!   Hey,   hey,   hey!   Shut de do!

124

Shut De Do

Have kids form two groups by either dividing the group in half or by separating guys to one group and girls to another.

For each verse, have the two groups sing and perform the parenthetical motions to the alternate lines. For the chorus and the bridge, have everyone sing and do the parenthetical motions together. For the coda, have kids repeat the chorus's actions.

Chorus:

Shut de do, keep out de devil. *(Clap on the words "shut" and "do"; then raise right arm and shake right fist four times.)*

Shut de do, keep de devil in de night! *(Clap on the words "shut" and "do"; then raise right arm and shake right fist four times.)*

Shut de do, keep out de devil. *(Clap on the words "shut" and "do"; then raise right arm and shake right fist four times.)*

Light a candle, everything's all right! *(Pretend to strike a match on the word "light," light an imaginary candle, and then give a thumbs up.)*

Light a candle, everything's all right! *(Pretend to strike a match on the word "light," light an imaginary candle, and then give a thumbs up.)*

1. Oh when I was a baby child *(group 1 kids motion as if rocking a baby),*
(Shut de do, keep out de devil.) *(Group 2 kids clap on the words "shut" and "do" and then raise right arms and shake right fists four times.)*
Good and bad was just a game. *(Group 1 kids motion thumbs up on "good," thumbs down on "bad," and shrug shoulders on "just a game.")*
(Shut de do, keep de devil in de night.) *(Group 2 kids clap on the words "shut" and "do" and then raise right arms and shake right fists four times.)*
Many years and many trials *(group 1 kids make fists and roll arms to the right),*
(Shut de do, keep out de devil.) *(Group 2 kids clap on the words "shut" and "do" and then raise right arms and shake right fists four times.)*
They proved to me they're not the same. *(Group 1 kids make fists and roll arms to the left.)*
(Shut de do, keep de devil in de night.) *(Group 2 kids clap on the words "shut" and "do" and then raise right arms and shake right fists four times.)*

2. Now Satan is an evil charmer *(group 2 kids place both hands together and make snake motions);*
(Shut de do, keep out de devil.) *(Group 1 kids clap on the words "shut" and "do" and then raise right arms and shake right fists four times.)*
He's hungry for a soul to hurt. *(Group 2 kids "snake" their hands right up to their throats and make a choking motion.)*
(Shut de do, keep de devil in de night.) *(Group 1 kids clap on the words "shut" and "do" and then raise right arms and shake right fists four times.)*
And without your holy armor *(group 2 kids make a cross by placing right arm perpendicular to left arm),*
(Shut de do, keep out de devil.) *(Group 1 kids clap on the words "shut" and "do" and then raise right arms and shake right fists.)*
He will eat you for dessert. *(Group 2 kids hold hands to stomachs and act "full.")*
(Shut de do, keep de devil in de night.) *(Group 1 kids clap on the words "shut" and "do" and then raise right arms and shake right fists.)*

Bridge:

(Groups sing and do the actions together.)

Hey, hey, hey! *(Wave arms overhead.)*

Shut de do! *(Clap on the words "shut" and "do.")*

Hey, hey, hey! *(Wave arms overhead.)*

Shut de do! *(Clap on the words "shut" and "do.")*

Hey, hey, hey! *(Wave arms overhead.)*

Shut de do! *(Clap on the words "shut" and "do.")*

Say a prayer, he won't be back no mo'! *(Hold hands as if praying; then hold both hands out as if pushing the devil away.)*

3. My mama used to sing this song. *(Group 1 kids hold hands around mouth, and sing in a high falsetto.)*

(Shut de do, keep out de devil.) *(Group 2 kids clap on the words "shut" and "do" and then raise right arms and shake right fists four times.)*

Oh, Papa used to sing it too. *(Group 1 kids hold hands around mouth, and sing in a low bass.)*

(Shut de do, keep de devil in de night.) *(Group 2 kids clap on the words "shut" and "do" and then raise right arms and shake right fists four times.)*

Jesus called and took them home *(group 1 kids cup hands near their ears for the words "Jesus called" and then raise arms up),*

(Shut de do, keep out de devil.) *(Group 2 kids clap on the words "shut" and "do" and then raise right arms and shake right fists four times.)*

And so I sing this song for you. *(Group 1 kids hold hands out to everyone.)*

(Shut de do, keep de devil in de night.) *(Group 2 kids clap on the words "shut" and "do" and then raise right arms and shake right fists four times.)*

VARIATIONS

● Sing a cappella, and make percussion instruments out of various surfaces in your room, such as wooden doors, metal cabinets, and plastic trash cans.

● Keep time during the chorus by opening and shutting a door.

● Sing in a dark room with lit candles.

● As you sing the song, travel throughout the church in search of a variety of doors to shut. Each time you see a different door, open and shut it to the beat.

Arnold and the Devil

SUMMARY: In this **just-for-fun game,** teenagers will throw two balls around a circle, trying to not get caught holding both.

PREPARATION: You'll need two sock balls, Nerf balls, or bean bags of different colors.

Have the teenagers stand in a circle. Hold up one of the balls. Say: **This ball is Arnold.** (Make up any name you wish, preferably not the name of anyone in your group. Or, for added fun, you could name this ball after each person in your group, changing the name after each round.)

Then say: **Begin passing Arnold around the circle, neighbor to neighbor. You may change directions, but you must pass Arnold only to a person next to you.** Let the ball get started going around the circle, and then hold up the second ball.

Say: **This ball is the devil. The devil can be thrown around the circle in any direction you wish. You are to try your hardest to not let the devil catch Arnold. If the devil does catch Arnold, begin again. Remember, Arnold can only be passed from neighbor to neighbor, while the devil can be thrown anywhere in the circle.**

Closin' the Door

SUMMARY: In this **just-for-fun game,** teenagers will become breathless trying to blow a ball off a table before a "door" closes.

PREPARATION: You'll need enough pingpong balls for half of your group, enough index cards for the other half, and several tables.

Have each person find a partner. Give one partner in each pair a pingpong ball and the other partner an index card. Have teenagers sit or kneel at opposite sides of the tables so that all of the pingpong partners are on one side and the index card partners are on the other side.

Say: **The pingpong partner will try to score a point by blowing the ping-pong ball off the opposite side of the table. If you're holding the index card, try to "shut the door" on the pingpong ball so your partner can't score a point. You must keep your index card even with the edge of the table. For each "save" with the index card, you'll score a point. When one partner gets five points, switch jobs.**

How Many Licks Does It Take?

SUMMARY: In this **learning game,** teenagers will try to get to the center of Tootsie Roll Pops first without biting them.

PREPARATION: You will need a Tootsie Roll Pop for each person.

Give each person a Tootsie Roll Pop, and tell kids not to open their lollipops until you say "go." Tell kids that the object of the game is to be the first person to get to the Tootsie Roll center without biting the lollipop. If someone bites the lollipop, he or she is disqualified. Play until the first person gets to the center without biting his or her lollipop. Then ask:

● **How was this game frustrating?**
● **How is the Tootsie Roll center like sin?**
● **How was trying not to bite the lollipop like facing temptation?**